Cuisinart Chef's Convection Toaster Oven Cookbook for Beginners

1000-Day Quick and Easy Recipes to Bake, Broil, Toast, Convection and More Impress Your Friends and Family with The Best Crispy and Healthy Meals

Dopa Rabins

© Copyright 2021 Dopa Rabins - All Rights Reserved.

In no way is it legal to reproduce, duplicate, or transmit any part of this document by either electronic means or in printed format. Recording of this publication is strictly prohibited, and any storage of this material is not allowed unless with written permission from the publisher. All rights reserved.

The information provided herein is stated to be truthful and consistent, in that any liability, regarding inattention or otherwise, by any usage or abuse of any policies, processes, or directions contained within is the solitary and complete responsibility of the recipient reader. Under no circumstances will any legal liability or blame be held against the publisher for any reparation, damages, or monetary loss due to the information herein, either directly or indirectly.

Respective authors own all copyrights not held by the publisher.

Legal Notice:

This book is copyright protected. This is only for personal use. You cannot amend, distribute, sell, use, quote or paraphrase any part of the content within this book without the consent of the author or copyright owner. Legal action will be pursued if this is breached.

Disclaimer Notice:

Please note the information contained within this document is for educational and entertainment purposes only. Every attempt has been made to provide accurate, up-to-date and reliable, complete information. No warranties of any kind are expressed or implied. Readers acknowledge that the author is not engaging in the rendering of legal, financial, medical or professional advice.

By reading this document, the reader agrees that under no circumstances are we responsible for any losses, direct or indirect, which are incurred as a result of the use of information contained within this document, including, but not limited to, errors, omissions, or inaccuracies.

Table of Contents

Introduction 5
Chapter 1: Cuisinart Chef's Convection Toaster Oven Basics 6
    What is Cuisinart Chef's Convection Toaster Oven? 6
    Features of Cuisinart Art Air Fryer Toaster Oven 6
    Cooking Functions 8
    Benefits of Using Cuisinart Chef's Convection Toaster Oven 9
    Tips 11
Chapter 2: Breakfast & Brunch 12
    Perfect Potato Casserole 12   Baked Peanut Butter Oatmeal 20
    Zucchini Breakfast Casserole 13   Breakfast Oatmeal Cake 21
    Easy Breakfast Bake 14   Moist Orange Bread Loaf 22
    Healthy Baked Oatmeal 15   Spinach Egg Bites 23
    Whole Wheat Carrot Bread 16   Baked Breakfast Quiche 24
    Ham Egg Muffins 17   Easy Cheese Egg Casserole 25
    Easy Egg Quiche 18   Omelet Egg Muffins 26
    Banana Oat Muffins 19
Chapter 3: Poultry 27
    Simple & Healthy Baked Chicken   Green Chili Chicken Noodle
    Breasts 27   Casserole 34
    Baked Spinach Cheese Chicken 28   Lemon Mustard Chicken 35
    Cheesy Bacon Chicken 29   Meatballs 36
    Zucchini Chicken Meatballs 30   Air Fryer Chicken Tenders 37
    Tasty Lemon Chicken 31   Sriracha Chicken Wings 38
    Meatballs 32   Garlic Chicken Wings 39
    Juicy Baked Chicken Breast 33   Easy BBQ Chicken Drumsticks 40
         Greek Chicken Breast 41
Chapter 4: Beef, Pork & Lamb 42
    Cheesy Pork Chops 42   Juicy & Tender Pork Chops 50
    Crispy Crusted Pork Chops 43   Baked Pork Ribs 51
    Perfect Beef Hash brown Bake 44   Meatballs 52
    Crunchy Parmesan Pork Chops 45   Flavorful Sirloin Steak 53
    Meatloaf 46   Tasty Breaded Pork Chops 54
    Delicious Lamb Patties 47   Air Fryer Juicy Pork Chops 55
    Meatballs 48   Meatballs 56
    Delicious Air Fryer Kebabs 49
Chapter 5: Fish & Seafood 57
    Italian Cod 57   Lemon Butter Shrimp 65
    Paprika Cod 58   Baked Buttery Shrimp 66
    Tender & Juicy Cajun Cod 59   Dijon Salmon Fillets 67
    Easy Baked Fish Fillet 60   Delicious Crab Cakes 68
    Perfect Crab Cakes 61   Miso White Fish Fillets 69
    Old Bay Seasoned Scallops 62   Spinach Scallops 70
    Cajun Red Snapper 63   Basil Tomato Salmon 71
    Flavorful Baked Halibut 64
Chapter 6: Vegetables & Side Dishes 72
    Cheese Herb Zucchini 72   Healthy Barley Bread 73

Baked Vegetables 74
Cheesy Broccoli Rice 75
Baked Cauliflower & Mushrooms . 76
Jalapeno Bread 77
Honey Corn Muffins 78
Tasty Butternut Squash 79
Brussels Sprouts & Sweet Potatoes. 80
Parmesan Baked Asparagus............. 81
Chili Lime Sweet Potatoes 82
Baked Potatoes Eggplant................. 83
Tasty Hassel Back Potatoes 84
Air Fried Eggplant Cubes 85
Lemon Garlic Brussels Sprouts....... 86

Chapter 7: Snacks & Appetizers 87
Cheesy Onion Dip.......................... 87
Air Fryer Walnuts 88
Spicy Brussels Sprouts..................... 89
Jalapeno Spinach Dip 90
Tasty Sweet Potato Fries 91
Habanero Chicken Wings 92
Air Fryer Radish Chips 93
Delicious Jalapeno Poppers 94
Air Fryer Cabbage Chips 95
Cheesy Brussels Sprouts.................. 96
Zucchini Coconut Bites 97
Yummy Turkey Jalapeno Poppers... 98
Air Fryer Nuts 99
Creamy Chicken Dip 100
Cheddar Dill Mushrooms............... 101

Chapter 8: Desserts 102
Easy Almond Butter Pumpkin Spice Cookies 102
Walnut Carrot Cake 103
Tasty Almond Macaroons.............. 104
Vanilla Peanut Butter Cake 105
Chocolate Cake.............................. 106
Mini Brownie Muffins 107
Vanilla Banana Brownies............... 108
Flavorful Coconut Cake 109
Almond Pecan Cookies 110
Orange Almond Muffins 111
Easy Lemon Cheesecake 112
Delicious Banana Cake 113
Flavors Pumpkin Custard 114
Tasty Gingersnap Cookies 115
Strawberry Muffins........................ 116

Conclusion 117

Introduction

A complete cookbook consisting of the easiest and tastiest recipes that you can attempt making with the Cuisinart Convection Toaster Oven today! Here's how to bake, grill and roast with your Cuisinart Convection Toaster Oven! Absolutely! This Cuisinart Chef's Convection Toaster Oven Cookbook turns your oven into an all-purpose cooking machine.

This Cuisinart Chef's Convection Toaster Oven Cookbook is comprised of a delicious collection of recipes that are suitable for all tastes. Each recipe is simple to make, full of flavor, and offers a healthier alternatives to traditionally fried foods. Throughout the pages of this cookbook, you will discover a variety of delicious recipes. These flavorful dishes are hand-picked to ensure you have a hearty collection of the best recipes on hand at all times. As a result, this Cuisinart Chef's Convection Toaster Oven Cookbook is the ultimate companion book to Cuisinart Chef's Convection Toaster Oven.

.

Chapter 1: Cuisinart Chef's Convection Toaster Oven Basics

What is Cuisinart Chef's Convection Toaster Oven?

The Cuisinart Chef's Convection Toaster Oven is an innovative and advanced cooking appliance used to perform different cooking techniques. As its name indicates that, it works as an oven toaster and air fryer these three different cooking techniques make it a unique cooking appliance.

The Cuisinart Chef's Convection Toaster Oven is working on 1800 watt and it is made up of a sturdy stainless steel body that gives sleek look to your Cuisinart oven. It is one of the multifunctional cooking appliances not only Air fry your food but also performs different operations like broil, toast, bake and warm, etc. Due to large capacity, you can toast 6 bread slices at a time, roast 4 pounds of chicken, and bake a 12-inch pizza.

It allows you to cook lots of different dishes like meat, poultry, fish, desserts, vegetables, and fruits. It runs on hot air circulation techniques in which hot air is circulating into the cooking chamber with the help of a convection fan situated at the top side of the oven. Using this technique Cuisinart Chef's Convection Toaster Oven cooks your food faster and evenly from all the sides. It fries your favourite French fries, chicken wings, and shrimp with very little oil or no oil. It is one of the healthier ways to prepare your favourite food faster.

Features of Cuisinart Art Air Fryer Toaster Oven

The Cuisinart Chef's Convection Toaster Oven is loaded with various features that make your daily cooking easiest, fastest, and safest way. These features are:

- **Power LED indicator**

The power light is illuminated continuously when the oven is in use. Continuous light illuminates indicates that when the oven is in use the exterior wall of the oven gets very hot.

- **On/Oven Timer Dial**

The timer dial is used to set the desire cooking time as per your recipe needs. The timer range is set in between 1 minute to 1 hour. When the timer is finished the oven is turned off. You cannot use the timer dial while using the toast function.

- **Temperature Dial**

The temperature dial helps you to set the desire temperature setting as per your recipe needs. The dial temperature range starts in between 150°F to 450°F.

- **Function Dial**

The function dial is used to select desire cooking functions from warm, broil, toast, bake, and air fry.

- **On/ Toast Timer dial**

This function allows you to select the desire toast shade from light, medium to dark. First set the function dialer at toast position then select the desired shade from the toasting dial. When the desire cooking cycle is completed the oven is power off automatically.

- **Light Button**

Using this button you can switch on the oven interior light to see the cooking process when the oven door is closed.

- **Pull Crumb Tray**

The Crumb tray is situated at the front bottom side of the oven. You can pull it out to easily clean for crumbs, bits, and pieces of foods fallen during baking or grilling

- **Air Fryer Basket**

It is recommended that while using the air fryer function you can use the air fryer basket seated into baking pan/drip tray to avoid the mess created during the air frying process.

- **Baking Pan/ Drip Tray**

As per your convenience, you can use it while you are roasting or baking your food. You can also use it while air frying your food to prevent spills residues.

- **Safety Auto OFF Door Switch**

The Cuisinart Chef's Convection Toaster Oven is equipped with a safety auto-off door switch which automatically shuts off the oven power supply if the oven door is opened.

- **Cord Storage**

At the backside of the oven, cord storage is given to store excess cord to keep your kitchen countertop clean and neat.

Cooking Functions

The Cuisinart Chef's Convection Toaster Oven comes with 5 different cooking functions these functions include:

1. **Warm**

This function is used to keep your food warm until it to be served. You can also reheat your leftover food or frozen food using this function. It keeps your food warm and makes your air fried food crisp again.

To use this function set your oven rack at rack 2 position. Then set the temperature dial at the warm position and function dial at warm. Select the desired time for warming your food using a timer dial. While the warming cycle is going on the power led illuminates and when the warming cycle has been completed the oven is automatically power off itself.

2. **Broil Convection Broil**

This function is used to broil your favourite burgers, melting cheese, and toppings spread over sandwiches. The combination of broil and convection gives a nice brown texture to your favourite meat and fish from all the sides.

While using this function first place the air fryer rack over a baking pan and set it into the rack to the position. Then set the function dial at broil convection position and temperature dial position to Toast/Broil position. Select the desire cooking time to start the actual broiling process. After finishing the cooking cycle the oven is automatically power off itself.

3. **Toast**

Using this function you can toast your favourite sandwich, bread, and warmed up your waffle.

To toast food first place your food in centre position at oven rack or baking pan and set it at rack position 2 for toasting purpose. Then set the function dial at toast position and temperature dial at Toast/Broil position. Turn the toast timer dial and select the desired shade from light, med, and dark. When the toasting cycle is complete the timer will ring and the oven automatically powers off.

4. **Bake Convection Bake**

This setting is ideal for baking your favourite foods. Using this setting you can bake casseroles, cakes, pastry, muffins, and cookies. With the help of convection fan hot air is blows fast into the cooking chamber and it gives you baking as well as browning results. You can make roast meat and make 8*11 inch pizza into baking pan.

To start baking first set the function dial at the bake convection bake position and select the desire temperature level with the help of the temperature dial. Turn and select the appropriate cooking time as per recipe needs. After finishing the baking cycle oven power off automatically. To get the best baking results always preheat your oven for 5 minutes prior.

5. **Air Fry**

This function is used to air fry your favourite foods like French fries, onion rings, chicken wings, and more. This is one of the healthy methods of frying your favourite food quickly and easily. It gives a nice crispy and crunchy texture to your food.

To air fry, your food first places the air fry rack into baking try and set it into rack position 2. Then set the function dial at air fry position and select desire temperature settings. Turn the timer dial and select the desired time as per recipe needs. When the cooking cycle is complete the oven is automatically powered off.

Benefits of Using Cuisinart Chef's Convection Toaster Oven

The Cuisinart Toaster oven is one of the multi-functional cooking appliances that work as an air fryer, oven, and toaster come with various benefits.

- **Cooks healthy Food**

Compare to the deep-frying method Cuisinart Chef's Convection Toaster Oven requires very little oil to cook your food. You cook a wide variety of fried food like

French fries, chicken wings, onion rings within a tablespoon of oil without compromising the taste and texture of food. It encourages you to change your daily eating habits towards healthy eating. Air fried food is one of the healthiest choices for daily cooking. They are lower in calories, fats, and some harmful compounds found in the traditional deep frying method.

- **Versatile Cooking Appliance**

The Cuisinart oven is performing operations of air fryer, oven, and toaster. You can use it for different operations like Air fry your French fries, broil meat or fish, toast bread or sandwich, bake your favourite cake and also keep your food warm. All these operations are made into a single appliance; you never need to buy a separate cooking appliance for each operation. It not only saves your time and energy but also saves your money.

- **Cooks your food faster**

The Cuisinart oven is loaded with a hot air circulation mechanism situated at the top side of the oven. It blows the hottest air with the help of a convection fan and cooks your food fast and evenly from all the sides. The oven consumes 1800 watt power to blow 450°F hot air which cooks your food quickly as compared to the traditional cooking method.

- **Cooks large quantity of food**

The Cuisinart oven is specially designed to hold more food. It comes with 2 rack positions and holds a large quantity of food at a time. The small frame and large interior allows you to bake a 12-inch pizza or air fry 3 pounds of chicken wings and also make a 12-inch pizza. Due to small and compact design, it also saves your kitchen countertop space.

- **Easy to clean**

The interior of the Cuisinart oven is coated with non-stick coating makes the daily cleaning process easy. The oven comes with a user manual you just need to follow the cleaning instructions as per given in the manual.

Tips

1. **Air Frying Tips**
   - Different types of oils are used while air frying your food. If you want mild flavour then use canola, vegetable, and grape-seed oil. If you want rich flavour then use olive oil during air fry.
   - Always flip the large food items like chicken cutlets during halfway of the cooking process. This will ensure that the food is cooked evenly from all the sides with a brown texture.
   - Do not crowd the food while air frying; this will affect the even cooking result, taste, and texture of food.
   - Cut food into even sizes, this will help to cook food more evenly and quickly.
2. **Broiling Tips**
   - To get a perfect broiling result always put the air fryer rack into the baking tray during the broiling process.
   - Use a sturdy metal pan during broiling. Do not use any glass while broiling even if the glass is strong.
   - To get a perfect broiling result to arrange food items in a single layer. This will ensure even cooking and browning results.
3. **Baking Tips**
   - A larger food item like chicken is placed into rack 1 position and while baking pizza use baking pan at rack 1 position.
   - Before start, the baking process always preheats your oven to get quick and perfect baking results.
4. **Toasting Tips**
   - Place your bread at the centre position of the oven to get even toasting results.
   - Always keep watch on your food from the oven window while toasting your food until how the oven cooks your food while toasting.

Chapter 2: Breakfast & Brunch

Perfect Potato Casserole

Preparation Time: 10 minutes
Cooking Time: 35 minutes
Serve: 6

Ingredients:

- 32 oz shredded potatoes
- 1/4 cup milk
- 1/4 cup butter, melted
- 1 cup cheddar cheese, shredded
- 10.5 oz cheddar cheese soup
- 2/3 cup sour cream
- 1/2 tsp onion powder
- 1/2 tsp garlic powder

Directions:

1. Fit the Cuisinart oven with the rack in position 1.
2. Spray 9*13-inch baking pan with cooking spray and set aside.
3. Add all ingredients into the greased baking pan and mix well.
4. Set to bake at 350 F for 40 minutes. After 5 minutes place the baking pan in the preheated oven.
5. Serve and enjoy.

Nutritional Value (Amount per Serving):

- Calories 341
- Fat 21.7 g
- Carbohydrates 28 g
- Sugar 2.5 g
- Protein 9.6 g
- Cholesterol 58 mg

Zucchini Breakfast Casserole

Preparation Time: 10 minutes

Cooking Time: 50 minutes

Serve: 8

Ingredients:

- 12 eggs
- 2 small zucchinis, shredded
- 1 lb ground sausage
- 3 tomatoes, sliced
- 3 tbsp coconut flour
- 1/4 cup coconut milk
- 1/4 tsp pepper
- 1/2 tsp salt

Directions:

1. Fit the Cuisinart oven with the rack in position 1.
2. Cook sausage in a pan until lightly brown.
3. Transfer sausage to a large mixing bowl.
4. Add coconut flour, milk, eggs, zucchini, pepper, and salt. Stir well.
5. Add eggs and whisk until well combined.
6. Pour bowl mixture into the greased casserole dish and top with tomato slices.
7. Set to bake at 350 F for 55 minutes, after 5 minutes, place the casserole dish in the oven.
8. Serve and enjoy.

Nutritional Value (Amount per Serving):

- Calories 330
- Fat 25 g
- Carbohydrates 5.7 g
- Sugar 2.7 g
- Protein 20.8 g
- Cholesterol 293 mg

Easy Breakfast Bake

Preparation Time: 10 minutes

Cooking Time: 45 minutes

Serve: 6

Ingredients:

- 10 eggs
- 10 bacon sliced, cooked, and crumbled
- 2 tomatoes, sliced
- 1 tbsp butter
- 3 cups baby spinach, chopped
- 1/2 tsp salt

Directions:

1. Fit the Cuisinart oven with the rack in position 1.
2. Melt butter in a pan.
3. Add spinach and cook until spinach wilted.
4. Whisk eggs and salt in a bowl. Add spinach and whisk well.
5. Pour egg mixture into the greased 9-inch baking dish. Top with bacon and tomatoes
6. Set to bake at 350 F for 50 minutes, after 5 minutes, place the baking dish in the oven.
7. Serve and enjoy.

Nutritional Value (Amount per Serving):

- Calories 266
- Fat 21 g
- Carbohydrates 2.7 g
- Sugar 1.7 g
- Protein 18.4 g
- Cholesterol 303 mg

Healthy Baked Oatmeal

Preparation Time: 10 minutes

Cooking Time: 20 minutes

Serve: 6

Ingredients:

- 1 egg
- 1/3 cup dried cranberries
- 1 tsp vanilla
- 1 1/2 tsp cinnamon
- 2 tbsp butter, melted
- 1/2 cup applesauce
- 1 1/2 cups milk
- 1 tsp baking powder
- 1/3 cup light brown sugar
- 2 cups old fashioned oats
- 1/4 tsp salt

Directions:

1. Fit the Cuisinart oven with the rack in position 1.
2. Grease 8*8-inch baking dish and set aside.
3. In a bowl, mix egg, vanilla, butter, applesauce, baking powder, cinnamon, brown sugar, oats, and salt.
4. Add milk and stir well.
5. Add cranberries and fold well.
6. Pour mixture into the prepared baking dish.
7. Set to bake at 350 F for 25 minutes. After 5 minutes place the baking dish in the preheated oven.
8. Serve and enjoy.

Nutritional Value (Amount per Serving):

- Calories 330
- Fat 9.3 g
- Carbohydrates 50.6 g
- Sugar 14.4 g
- Protein 9.7 g
- Cholesterol 42 mg

Whole Wheat Carrot Bread

Preparation Time: 10 minutes

Cooking Time: 50 minutes

Serve: 10

Ingredients:

- 1 egg
- 3/4 cup whole wheat flour
- 1 cup carrots, shredded
- 3/4 tsp vanilla
- 3/4 cup all-purpose flour
- 1/2 cup brown sugar
- 1 tsp baking powder
- 1/2 tsp nutmeg
- 1 1/2 tsp cinnamon
- 3/4 cup yogurt
- 3 tbsp vegetable oil
- 1 tsp baking soda

Directions:

1. Fit the Cuisinart oven with the rack in position 1.
2. In a large bowl, mix all dry ingredients and set aside.
3. In a separate bowl, whisk the egg with vanilla, sugar, yogurt, and oil.
4. Add carrots and fold well.
5. Add dry ingredient mixture and stir until just combined.
6. Pour mixture into the 9*5-inch greased loaf pan.
7. Set to bake at 350 F for 55 minutes, after 5 minutes, place the loaf pan in the oven.
8. Slice and serve.

Nutritional Value (Amount per Serving):

- Calories 159
- Fat 5 g
- Carbohydrates 24.4 g
- Sugar 9 g
- Protein 3.7 g
- Cholesterol 17 mg

Ham Egg Muffins

Preparation Time: 10 minutes
Cooking Time: 20 minutes
Serve: 12

Ingredients:

- 12 eggs
- 2 cups ham, diced
- 1 3/4 cup cheddar cheese, shredded
- 1/2 pepper
- 1/2 tsp salt

Directions:

1. Fit the Cuisinart oven with the rack in position 1.
2. Spray 12-cups muffin tin with cooking spray and set aside.
3. In a bowl, whisk eggs with pepper and salt.
4. Stir in cheddar cheese and ham.
5. Pour egg mixture into prepared muffin tin.
6. Set to bake at 375 F for 25 minutes, after 5 minutes, place the muffin tin in the oven.
7. Serve and enjoy.

Nutritional Value (Amount per Serving):

- Calories 166
- Fat 11.8 g
- Carbohydrates 1.5 g
- Sugar 0.4 g
- Protein 13.4 g
- Cholesterol 194 mg

Easy Egg Quiche

Preparation Time: 10 minutes

Cooking Time: 45 minutes

Serve: 6

Ingredients:

- 8 eggs
- 4 tbsp butter, melted
- 6 oz cream cheese
- 6 oz cheddar cheese, shredded

Directions:

1. Fit the Cuisinart oven with the rack in position 1.
2. Add eggs, cheese, butter, and cream cheese into the bowl and whisk until well combined.
3. Pour egg mixture into the greased pie dish.
4. Set to bake at 325 F for 50 minutes, after 5 minutes, place the pie dish in the oven.
5. Serve and enjoy.

Nutritional Value (Amount per Serving):

- Calories 365
- Fat 32.8 g
- Carbohydrates 1.6 g
- Sugar 0.7 g
- Protein 16.7 g
- Cholesterol 300 mg

Banana Oat Muffins

Preparation Time: 10 minutes
Cooking Time: 25 minutes
Serve: 6

Ingredients:

- 1 egg
- 2 tbsp butter, melted
- 1/2 tsp cinnamon
- 1 tsp vanilla
- 2 tbsp yogurt
- 1 1/2 cup oats
- 1 tsp baking powder
- 2 ripe bananas, mashed

Directions:

1. Fit the Cuisinart oven with the rack in position 1.
2. Line the muffin tray with cupcake liners and set aside.
3. In a bowl, whisk the egg with banana, yogurt, vanilla, cinnamon, baking powder, and butter.
4. Add oats and mix well.
5. Pour mixture into the prepared muffin tray.
6. Set to bake at 350 F for 30 minutes. After 5 minutes place the muffin tray in the preheated oven.
7. Serve and enjoy.

Nutritional Value (Amount per Serving):

- Calories 164
- Fat 6.1 g
- Carbohydrates 23.9 g
- Sugar 5.5 g
- Protein 4.4 g
- Cholesterol 38 mg

Baked Peanut Butter Oatmeal

Preparation Time: 10 minutes

Cooking Time: 35 minutes

Serve: 4

Ingredients:

- 2 cups old fashioned oats
- 2 tsp vanilla
- 1/4 cup maple syrup
- 1/2 cup peanut butter
- 1 3/4 cup almond milk
- 1/4 tsp salt

Directions:

1. Fit the Cuisinart oven with the rack in position 1.
2. In a mixing bowl, whisk together almond milk, vanilla, maple syrup, peanut butter, and salt.
3. Add oats and stir to mix.
4. Pour oats mixture into the greased baking dish.
5. Set to bake at 375 F for 40 minutes, after 5 minutes, place the baking dish in the oven.
6. Serve and enjoy.

Nutritional Value (Amount per Serving):

- Calories 800
- Fat 46.5 g
- Carbohydrates 79.3 g
- Sugar 20.6 g
- Protein 20.5 g
- Cholesterol 0 mg

Breakfast Oatmeal Cake

Preparation Time: 10 minutes
Cooking Time: 25 minutes
Serve: 8

Ingredients:

- 2 eggs
- 1 tbsp coconut oil
- 3 tbsp yogurt
- 1/2 tsp baking powder
- 1 tsp cinnamon
- 1 tsp vanilla
- 3 tbsp honey
- 1/2 tsp baking soda
- 1 apple, peel & chopped
- 1 cup oats

Directions:

1. Fit the Cuisinart oven with the rack in position 1.
2. Line baking dish with parchment paper and set aside.
3. Add 3/4 cup oats and remaining ingredients into the blender and blend until smooth.
4. Add remaining oats and stir well.
5. Pour mixture into the prepared baking dish.
6. Set to bake at 350 F for 30 minutes. After 5 minutes place the baking dish in the preheated oven.
7. Slice and serve.

Nutritional Value (Amount per Serving):

- Calories 114
- Fat 3.6 g
- Carbohydrates 18.2 g
- Sugar 10 g
- Protein 3.2 g
- Cholesterol 41 mg

Moist Orange Bread Loaf

Preparation Time: 10 minutes

Cooking Time: 50 minutes

Serve: 10

Ingredients:

- 4 eggs
- 4 oz butter, softened
- 1 cup of orange juice
- 1 orange zest, grated
- 1 cup of sugar
- 2 tsp baking powder
- 2 cups all-purpose flour
- 1 tsp vanilla

Directions:

1. Fit the Cuisinart oven with the rack in position 1.
2. In a large bowl, whisk eggs and sugar until creamy.
3. Whisk in vanilla, butter, orange juice, and orange zest.
4. Add flour and baking powder and mix until combined.
5. Pour batter into the greased 9*5-inch loaf pan.
6. Set to bake at 350 F for 55 minutes, after 5 minutes, place the loaf pan in the oven.
7. Slice and serve.

Nutritional Value (Amount per Serving):

- Calories 286
- Fat 11.3 g
- Carbohydrates 42.5 g
- Sugar 22.4 g
- Protein 5.1 g
- Cholesterol 90 mg

Spinach Egg Bites

Preparation Time: 10 minutes
Cooking Time: 20 minutes
Serve: 12

Ingredients:

- 8 eggs
- 1/4 cup almond milk
- 1/4 cup green onion, chopped
- 1 cup spinach, chopped
- 1 cup roasted red peppers, chopped
- 1/2 tsp salt

Directions:

1. Fit the Cuisinart oven with the rack in position 1.
2. Spray 12-cups muffin tin with cooking spray and set aside.
3. In a bowl, whisk eggs with milk and salt.
4. Add spinach, green onion, and red peppers to the egg mixture and stir to combine.
5. Pour egg mixture into the greased muffin tin.
6. Set to bake at 350 F for 25 minutes, after 5 minutes, place muffin tin in the oven.
7. Serve and enjoy.

Nutritional Value (Amount per Serving):

- Calories 59
- Fat 4.2 g
- Carbohydrates 1.7 g
- Sugar 1.1 g
- Protein 4.1 g
- Cholesterol 109 mg

Baked Breakfast Quiche

Preparation Time: 10 minutes

Cooking Time: 45 minutes

Serve: 6

Ingredients:

- 6 eggs
- 1 cup milk
- 1 cup cheddar cheese, grated
- 1 cup tomatoes, chopped
- Pepper
- Salt

Directions:

1. Fit the Cuisinart oven with the rack in position 1.
2. In a bowl, whisk eggs with cheese, milk, pepper, and salt. Stir in tomatoes.
3. Pour egg mixture into the greased pie dish.
4. Set to bake at 350 F for 50 minutes, after 5 minutes, place the pie dish in the oven.
5. Serve and enjoy.

Nutritional Value (Amount per Serving):

- Calories 165
- Fat 11.5 g
- Carbohydrates 3.8 g
- Sugar 3.1 g
- Protein 11.8 g
- Cholesterol 187 mg

Easy Cheese Egg Casserole

Preparation Time: 10 minutes

Cooking Time: 40 minutes

Serve: 10

Ingredients:

- 12 eggs
- 8 oz cheddar cheese, shredded
- 1/3 cup milk
- 1/4 tsp pepper
- 1 tsp salt

Directions:

1. Fit the Cuisinart oven with the rack in position 1.
2. Spray 9*13-inch casserole dish with cooking spray and set aside.
3. In a bowl, whisk eggs with milk, pepper, and salt.
4. Add shredded cheese and stir well.
5. Pour egg mixture into the prepared casserole dish.
6. Set to bake at 350 F for 45 minutes. After 5 minutes place the casserole dish in the preheated oven.
7. Serve and enjoy.

Nutritional Value (Amount per Serving):

- Calories 171
- Fat 12.9 g
- Carbohydrates 1.1 g
- Sugar 0.9 g
- Protein 12.6 g
- Cholesterol 221 mg

Omelet Egg Muffins

Preparation Time: 10 minutes
Cooking Time: 20 minutes
Serve: 12

Ingredients:

- 12 eggs, lightly beaten
- 1 cup tomatoes, chopped
- 4 tbsp water
- 1 tsp Italian seasoning
- 1 cup fresh spinach, chopped
- 1/2 tsp pepper
- 1/4 tsp salt

Directions:

1. Fit the Cuisinart oven with the rack in position 1.
2. Spray 12-cups muffin tin with cooking spray and set aside.
3. Whisk eggs in a bowl with water, Italian seasoning, pepper, and salt.
4. Add spinach and tomatoes to the egg mixture and whisk well.
5. Pour egg mixture into the greased muffin tin.
6. Set to bake at 350 F for 25 minutes, after 5 minutes, place muffin tin in the oven.
7. Serve and enjoy.

Nutritional Value (Amount per Serving):

- Calories 68
- Fat 4.5 g
- Carbohydrates 1.1 g
- Sugar 0.8 g
- Protein 5.8 g
- Cholesterol 164 mg

Chapter 3: Poultry

Simple & Healthy Baked Chicken Breasts

Preparation Time: 10 minutes

Cooking Time: 20 minutes

Serve: 6

Ingredients:

- 6 chicken breasts, skinless & boneless
- 1/4 tsp paprika
- 1 tsp Italian seasoning
- 2 tbsp olive oil
- 1/4 tsp pepper
- 1/2 tsp seasoning salt

Directions:

1. Fit the Cuisinart oven with the rack in position 1.
2. Brush chicken with oil and season with paprika, Italian seasoning, pepper, and salt.
3. Place chicken breasts into the baking dish.
4. Set to bake at 400 F for 25 minutes. After 5 minutes place the baking dish in the preheated oven.
5. Serve and enjoy.

Nutritional Value (Amount per Serving):

- Calories 320
- Fat 15.7 g
- Carbohydrates 0.2 g
- Sugar 0.1 g
- Protein 42.3 g
- Cholesterol 130 mg

Baked Spinach Cheese Chicken

Preparation Time: 10 minutes

Cooking Time: 20 minutes

Serve: 2

Ingredients:

- 2 chicken breasts, boneless & skinless
- 1/2 tsp garlic powder
- 1/4 cup sun-dried tomatoes, chopped
- 1/4 cup cheddar cheese, shredded
- 3 oz cream cheese
- 2 cups fresh spinach, chopped
- 3/4 tsp pepper
- 3/4 tsp salt

Directions:

1. Fit the Cuisinart oven with the rack in position 1.
2. Slice the chicken breasts into the half and place them into the baking dish. Season with pepper and salt.
3. Cook spinach in the pan until wilted.
4. In a bowl, mix spinach, garlic powder, tomatoes, cheddar cheese, and cream cheese.
5. Spread spinach mixture on top of chicken breasts.
6. Set to bake at 425 F for 25 minutes. After 5 minutes place the baking dish in the preheated oven.
7. Serve and enjoy.

Nutritional Value (Amount per Serving):

- Calories 498
- Fat 30.5 g
- Carbohydrates 4.3 g
- Sugar 1.1 g
- Protein 50.2 g
- Cholesterol 192 mg

Cheesy Bacon Chicken

Preparation Time: 10 minutes

Cooking Time: 30 minutes

Serve: 4

Ingredients:

- 4 chicken breasts, sliced in half
- 1 cup cheddar cheese, shredded
- 8 bacon slices, cooked & chopped
- 6 oz cream cheese
- Pepper
- Salt

Directions:

1. Fit the Cuisinart oven with the rack in position 1.
2. Place season chicken with pepper and salt and place it into the greased baking dish.
3. Add cream cheese and bacon on top of chicken.
4. Sprinkle shredded cheddar cheese on top of chicken.
5. Set to bake at 400 F for 35 minutes. After 5 minutes place the baking dish in the preheated oven.
6. Serve and enjoy.

Nutritional Value (Amount per Serving):

- Calories 745
- Fat 50.9 g
- Carbohydrates 2.1 g
- Sugar 0.2 g
- Protein 66.6 g
- Cholesterol 248 mg

Zucchini Chicken Meatballs

Preparation Time: 10 minutes

Cooking Time: 18 minutes

Serve: 6

Ingredients:

- 1 lb ground chicken
- 1 tbsp basil, chopped
- 1/3 cup coconut flour
- 2 cups zucchini, grated
- 1 tsp dried oregano
- 1 tbsp garlic, minced
- 1 tbsp nutritional yeast
- 1 tsp cumin
- 1 tbsp dried onion flakes
- 2 eggs, lightly beaten
- Pepper
- Salt

Directions:

1. Fit the Cuisinart oven with the rack in position 1.
2. Add all ingredients into the mixing bowl and mix until well combined.
3. Make small balls from the meat mixture and place them into the baking pan.
4. Set to bake at 400 F for 23 minutes. After 5 minutes place the baking pan in the preheated oven.
5. Serve and enjoy.

Nutritional Value (Amount per Serving):

- Calories 215
- Fat 8.5 g
- Carbohydrates 7.6 g
- Sugar 1.5 g
- Protein 26.5 g
- Cholesterol 122 mg

Tasty Lemon Chicken

Preparation Time: 10 minutes

Cooking Time: 15 minutes

Serve: 1

Ingredients:

- 1 chicken breast, boneless and skinless
- 1 fresh lemon juice
- 1 fresh lemon, sliced
- 1/2 tbsp Italian seasoning
- Pepper
- Salt

Directions:

1. Fit the Cuisinart oven with the rack in position 1.
2. Season chicken with Italian season, pepper, and salt.
3. Place chicken breast in baking dish.
4. Pour lemon juice over chicken and arrange lemon slices on top of chicken.
5. Set to bake at 350 F for 20 minutes. After 5 minutes place the baking dish in the preheated oven.
6. Serve and enjoy.

Nutritional Value (Amount per Serving):

- Calories 178
- Fat 5.4 g
- Carbohydrates 7.2 g
- Sugar 3.1 g
- Protein 24.8 g
- Cholesterol 77 mg

Meatballs

Preparation Time: 10 minutes
Cooking Time: 25 minutes
Serve: 6

Ingredients:

- 1 lb ground turkey
- 1 egg, lightly beaten
- 2 tbsp basil, chopped
- 2 tbsp coconut flour
- 1 tsp olive oil
- 1/2 tsp ground ginger
- 1/2 tsp salt

Directions:

1. Fit the Cuisinart oven with the rack in position 1.
2. In a bowl, mix turkey, basil, coconut flour, olive oil, ginger, egg, and salt until well combined.
3. Make small balls from the meat mixture and place it into the parchment-lined baking pan.
4. Set to bake at 375 F for 30 minutes. After 5 minutes place the baking pan in the preheated oven.
5. Serve and enjoy.

Nutritional Value (Amount per Serving):

- Calories 185
- Fat 10.5 g
- Carbohydrates 2.9 g
- Sugar 0.4 g
- Protein 22.3 g
- Cholesterol 104 mg

Juicy Baked Chicken Breast

Preparation Time: 10 minutes

Cooking Time: 25 minutes

Serve: 4

Ingredients:

- 4 chicken breasts
- 1 tbsp fresh parsley, chopped
- 1/4 tsp red pepper flakes
- 1/2 tsp black pepper
- 1 tsp Italian seasoning
- 2 tbsp olive oil
- 1/4 cup balsamic vinegar
- 1 tsp kosher salt

Directions:

1. Fit the Cuisinart oven with the rack in position 1.
2. Place chicken breasts into the mixing bowl.
3. Mix together remaining ingredients and pour over chicken breasts and coat well and let marinate for 30 minutes.
4. Arrange marinated chicken breasts into a greased baking dish.
5. Set to bake at 425 F for 30 minutes. After 5 minutes place the baking dish in the preheated oven.
6. Slice and serve.

Nutritional Value (Amount per Serving):

- Calories 345
- Fat 18.2 g
- Carbohydrates 0.6 g
- Sugar 0.2 g
- Protein 42.3 g
- Cholesterol 131 mg

Green Chili Chicken Noodle Casserole

Preparation Time: 10 minutes

Cooking Time: 30 minutes

Serve: 6

Ingredients:

- 3 cups cooked chicken, shredded
- 4 oz can green chilies
- 1/3 cup parmesan cheese, shredded
- 3 cups cheddar cheese, shredded
- 1 1/3 cups milk
- 10.5 oz cream of chicken soup
- 1 tsp chili powder
- 1 onion, diced
- 1/3 cup bell pepper, diced
- 3 tbsp butter
- 3 cups shell noodles, uncooked
- 1/2 tsp salt

Directions:

1. Fit the Cuisinart oven with the rack in position 1.
2. Cook noodles according to the packet instructions and drain well.
3. Melt butter in a pan over medium heat.
4. Add bell pepper and onion and sauté for 5 minutes. Stir in chili powder and salt.
5. In a large bowl, mix chicken soup, parmesan cheese, 2 cups cheddar cheese, milk, and sautéed onion bell pepper. Stir in green chilies, noodles, and chicken.
6. Pour mixture into the greased 9*13-inch baking dish and top with remaining cheese.
7. Set to bake at 375 F for 35 minutes. After 5 minutes place the baking dish in the preheated oven.
8. Serve and enjoy.

Nutritional Value (Amount per Serving):

- Calories 560
- Fat 32.6 g
- Carbohydrates 23.9 g
- Sugar 5 g
- Protein 42.2 g
- Cholesterol 156 mg

Lemon Mustard Chicken

Preparation Time: 10 minutes
Cooking Time: 20 minutes
Serve: 4

Ingredients:

- 1 lbs chicken tenders
- 1 garlic clove, minced
- 1/2 oz fresh lemon juice
- 1/2 tsp pepper
- 2 tbsp fresh tarragon, chopped
- 1/2 cup whole grain mustard
- 1/2 tsp paprika
- 1/4 tsp kosher salt

Directions:

1. Fit the Cuisinart oven with the rack in position 1.
2. Add all ingredients except chicken to the large bowl and mix well.
3. Add chicken to the bowl and stir until well coated.
4. Place chicken in a baking dish.
5. Set to bake at 425 F for 25 minutes. After 5 minutes place the baking dish in the preheated oven.
6. Serve and enjoy.

Nutritional Value (Amount per Serving):

- Calories 242
- Fat 9.5 g
- Carbohydrates 3.1 g
- Sugar 0.1 g
- Protein 33.2 g
- Cholesterol 101 mg

Meatballs

Preparation Time: 10 minutes
Cooking Time: 20 minutes
Serve: 4

Ingredients:

- 1 lb ground turkey
- 1/4 cup basil, chopped
- 3 tbsp scallions, chopped
- 1 egg, lightly beaten
- 1/2 cup almond flour
- 1/2 tsp red pepper, crushed
- 1 tbsp lemongrass, chopped
- 1 1/2 tbsp fish sauce
- 2 garlic cloves, minced

Directions:

1. Fit the Cuisinart oven with the rack in position 2.
2. Line the air fryer basket with parchment paper.
3. Add all ingredients into a large bowl and mix until well combined.
4. Make small balls from meat mixture and place in the air fryer basket then place the air fryer basket in the baking pan.
5. Place a baking pan on the oven rack. Set to air fry at 380 F for 20 minutes.
6. Serve and enjoy.

Nutritional Value (Amount per Serving):

- Calories 269
- Fat 15.4 g
- Carbohydrates 3.4 g
- Sugar 1.3 g
- Protein 33.9 g
- Cholesterol 157 mg

Air Fryer Chicken Tenders

Preparation Time: 10 minutes

Cooking Time: 16 minutes

Serve: 4

Ingredients:

- 1 lb chicken tenders
- For rub:
- 1/2 tbsp dried thyme
- 1 tbsp garlic powder
- 1 tbsp paprika
- 1/2 tbsp onion powder
- 1/2 tsp cayenne pepper
- Pepper
- Salt

Directions:

1. Fit the Cuisinart oven with the rack in position 2.
2. In a bowl, add all rub ingredients and mix well.
3. Add chicken tenders into the bowl and coat well.
4. Place chicken tenders in the air fryer basket then place an air fryer basket in the baking pan.
5. Place a baking pan on the oven rack. Set to air fry at 370 F for 16 minutes.
6. Serve and enjoy.

Nutritional Value (Amount per Serving):

- Calories 232
- Fat 8.7 g
- Carbohydrates 3.6 g
- Sugar 1 g
- Protein 33.6 g
- Cholesterol 101 mg

Sriracha Chicken Wings

Preparation Time: 10 minutes
Cooking Time: 30 minutes
Serve: 4

Ingredients:

- 1 lb chicken wings
- 2 tbsp sriracha sauce
- 1/4 cup honey
- 1 tbsp butter
- 1 1/2 tbsp soy sauce
- Pepper
- Salt

Directions:

1. Fit the Cuisinart oven with the rack in position 2.
2. Season chicken wings with pepper and salt.
3. Add chicken wings to the air fryer basket then place an air fryer basket in the baking pan.
4. Place a baking pan on the oven rack. Set to air fry at 360 F for 30 minutes.
5. Meanwhile, add butter, soy sauce, sriracha sauce, and honey in a saucepan and cook for 3 minutes.
6. Add chicken wings into the bowl.
7. Pour sauce over chicken wings and toss until well coated.
8. Serve and enjoy.

Nutritional Value (Amount per Serving):

- Calories 359
- Fat 16.3 g
- Carbohydrates 18.4 g
- Sugar 18 g
- Protein 33.3 g
- Cholesterol 114 mg

Garlic Chicken Wings

Preparation Time: 10 minutes
Cooking Time: 25 minutes
Serve: 2

Ingredients:

- 1 lb chicken wings
- 2 tbsp butter, melted
- 1 tbsp garlic, minced

Directions:

1. Fit the Cuisinart oven with the rack in position 2.
2. In a large bowl, mix butter and garlic. Add chicken wings and toss to coat.
3. Add marinated chicken wings to the air fryer basket then place an air fryer basket in the baking pan.
4. Place a baking pan on the oven rack. Set to air fry at 360 F for 25 minutes.
5. Serve and enjoy.

Nutritional Value (Amount per Serving):

- Calories 539
- Fat 28.4 g
- Carbohydrates 1.4 g
- Sugar 0.1 g
- Protein 66 g
- Cholesterol 232 mg

Easy BBQ Chicken Drumsticks

Preparation Time: 10 minutes

Cooking Time: 25 minutes

Serve: 4

Ingredients:

- 4 chicken drumsticks
- 1/4 tsp paprika
- 1/2 tsp garlic powder
- 2 tbsp olive oil
- 1/2 cup BBQ sauce
- 1/2 tsp onion powder
- Pepper
- Salt

Directions:

1. Fit the Cuisinart oven with the rack in position 2.
2. In a mixing bowl, add chicken drumsticks, onion powder, garlic powder, olive oil, paprika, pepper, and salt and toss well.
3. Add chicken drumsticks to the air fryer basket then place an air fryer basket in baking pan.
4. Place a baking pan on the oven rack. Set to air fry at 400 F for 20 minutes.
5. Brush chicken drumsticks with BBQ sauce and air fry for 5 minutes.
6. Serve and enjoy.

Nutritional Value (Amount per Serving):

- Calories 187
- Fat 9.7 g
- Carbohydrates 11.9 g
- Sugar 8.4 g
- Protein 12.8 g
- Cholesterol 40 mg

Greek Chicken Breast

Preparation Time: 10 minutes
Cooking Time: 25 minutes
Serve: 4

Ingredients:

- 4 chicken breasts, skinless & boneless
- 1 tbsp olive oil

For rub:

- 1 tsp oregano
- 1 tsp thyme
- 1 tsp parsley
- 1 tsp onion powder
- 1 tsp basil
- Pepper
- Salt

Directions:

1. Fit the Cuisinart oven with the rack in position 2.
2. Brush chicken with olive oil.
3. In a small bowl, mix together all rub ingredients and rub all over the chicken breasts.
4. Place chicken into the air fryer basket then places the air fryer basket in the baking pan.
5. Place a baking pan on the oven rack. Set to air fry at 390 F for 25 minutes.
6. Serve and enjoy.

Nutritional Value (Amount per Serving):

- Calories 312
- Fat 14.4 g
- Carbohydrates 0.9 g
- Sugar 0.2 g
- Protein 42.4 g
- Cholesterol 130 mg

Chapter 4: Beef, Pork & Lamb

Cheesy Pork Chops

Preparation Time: 10 minutes
Cooking Time: 40 minutes
Serve: 4

Ingredients:

- 4 pork chops
- 1/2 tsp garlic powder
- 1/2 tsp pepper
- 1/2 tsp dried parsley
- 1/4 tsp paprika
- 1/4 cup Italian seasoned breadcrumbs
- 1/2 cup parmesan cheese, grated
- 1 tbsp olive oil
- Salt

Directions:

1. Fit the Cuisinart oven with the rack in position 1.
2. In a shallow dish, mix cheese, paprika, breadcrumbs, parsley, pepper, garlic powder, and salt.
3. Brush pork chops with oil and coat with parmesan cheese.
4. Place coated pork chops into the baking dish.
5. Set to bake at 350 F for 45 minutes. After 5 minutes place the baking dish in the preheated oven.
6. Serve and enjoy.

Nutritional Value (Amount per Serving):

- Calories 353
- Fat 26.2 g
- Carbohydrates 6 g
- Sugar 0.5 g
- Protein 22.8 g
- Cholesterol 77 mg

Crispy Crusted Pork Chops

Preparation Time: 10 minutes
Cooking Time: 15 minutes
Serve: 2

Ingredients:

- 2 pork chops, bone-in
- 1 cup pork rinds, crushed
- 1/2 tsp parsley
- 1 tbsp olive oil
- 1/2 tsp garlic powder
- 1/2 tsp onion powder
- 1/2 tsp paprika

Directions:

1. Fit the Cuisinart oven with the rack in position 2.
2. In a large bowl, mix pork rinds, garlic powder, onion powder, parsley, and paprika.
3. Brush pork chops with oil and coat with pork rind mixture.
4. place coated pork chops in air fryer basket then place air fryer basket in baking pan.
5. Place a baking pan on the oven rack. Set to air fry at 400 F for 15 minutes.
6. Serve and enjoy.

Nutritional Value (Amount per Serving):

- Calories 413
- Fat 32.7 g
- Carbohydrates 1.3 g
- Sugar 0.4 g
- Protein 28.5 g
- Cholesterol 92 mg

Perfect Beef Hash brown Bake

Preparation Time: 10 minutes

Cooking Time: 40 minutes

Serve: 4

Ingredients:

- 1 lb ground beef
- 2 cups cheddar cheese, shredded
- 1 cup milk
- 10 oz can cream of mushroom soup
- 30 oz frozen shredded hash browns
- 1 tsp garlic powder
- 1 tbsp onion, minced
- Pepper
- Salt

Directions:

1. Fit the Cuisinart oven with the rack in position 1.
2. In a pan, brown ground beef with garlic powder, onion, pepper, and salt. Drain.
3. In a bowl, mix meat, shredded cheese, milk, soup, and hash browns.
4. Pour meat mixture into the greased 9*13-inch baking dish.
5. Set to bake at 350 F for 45 minutes. After 5 minutes place the baking dish in the preheated oven.
6. Serve and enjoy.

Nutritional Value (Amount per Serving):

- Calories 514
- Fat 28.3 g
- Carbohydrates 11.4 g
- Sugar 4.8 g
- Protein 51.6 g
- Cholesterol 168 mg

Crunchy Parmesan Pork Chops

Preparation Time: 10 minutes

Cooking Time: 10 minutes

Serve: 4

Ingredients:

- 4 pork chops, boneless
- 2 tbsp olive oil
- 1/4 tsp pepper
- 1/2 tsp garlic powder
- 1 tsp dried parsley
- 1/4 tsp smoked paprika
- 2 tbsp breadcrumbs
- 1/4 cup parmesan cheese, grated

Directions:

1. Fit the Cuisinart oven with the rack in position 1.
2. In a shallow dish, mix breadcrumbs, paprika, parmesan cheese, garlic powder, parsley, and pepper.
3. Brush pork chops with oil and coat with breadcrumb mixture.
4. Place coated pork chops into the baking pan.
5. Set to bake at 450 F for 15 minutes. After 5 minutes place the baking pan in the preheated oven.
6. Serve and enjoy.

Nutritional Value (Amount per Serving):

- Calories 350
- Fat 28.3 g
- Carbohydrates 3.1 g
- Sugar 0.3 g
- Protein 20.4 g
- Cholesterol 73 mg

Meatloaf

Preparation Time: 10 minutes
Cooking Time: 60 minutes
Serve: 8

Ingredients:

- 3 eggs
- 45 Ritz crackers, crushed
- 1 1/2 lbs lean ground beef
- 1/2 cup milk
- 4 oz sharp cheddar cheese, shredded
- 1/4 cup green pepper, diced
- 1/2 cup onion, chopped
- 1/4 tsp black pepper
- 1 tsp salt

For topping:

- 1 tsp yellow mustard
- 1/2 cup brown sugar
- 1/2 cup ketchup

Directions:

1. Fit the Cuisinart oven with the rack in position 1.
2. In a small bowl, mix together all topping ingredients and set aside.
3. In a mixing bowl, beat the eggs then add cheese, green pepper, onion, cracker crumbs, milk pepper, and salt. Stir well to combine.
4. Add ground meat and mix well.
5. Make a loaf of meat mixture and place it into the parchment-lined baking pan.
6. Set to bake at 350 F for 35 minutes. After 5 minutes place the baking pan in the preheated oven.
7. Spread topping mixture on top of the meatloaf and bake for 30 minutes more.
8. Slice and serve.

Nutritional Value (Amount per Serving):

- Calories 316
- Fat 12.7 g
- Carbohydrates 17 g
- Sugar 13.7 g
- Protein 32.7 g
- Cholesterol 154 mg

Delicious Lamb Patties

Preparation Time: 10 minutes
Cooking Time: 15 minutes
Serve: 4

Ingredients:

- 1 lb ground lamb
- 1 tsp ground coriander
- 1 tsp ground cumin
- 1/4 cup fresh parsley, chopped
- 1/4 cup onion, minced
- 1 tbsp garlic, minced
- 1/4 tsp cayenne pepper
- 1/2 tsp ground allspice
- 1 tsp ground cinnamon
- 1/4 tsp pepper
- 1 tsp kosher salt

Directions:

1. Fit the Cuisinart oven with the rack in position 1.
2. Add all ingredients into the mixing bowl and mix until well combined.
3. Make small patties from meat mixture and place onto the parchment-lined baking pan.
4. Set to bake at 450 F for 20 minutes. After 5 minutes place the baking pan in the preheated oven.
5. Serve and enjoy.

Nutritional Value (Amount per Serving):

- Calories 223
- Fat 8.5 g
- Carbohydrates 2.6 g
- Sugar 0.4 g
- Protein 32.3 g
- Cholesterol 102 mg

Meatballs

Preparation Time: 10 minutes
Cooking Time: 20 minutes
Serve: 4

Ingredients:

- 1 egg, lightly beaten
- 1 lb ground lamb
- 2 tbsp fresh parsley, chopped
- 1 tbsp garlic, minced
- 1/4 tsp red pepper flakes
- 1 tsp ground cumin
- 2 tsp fresh oregano, chopped
- 1/4 tsp pepper
- 1 tsp kosher salt

Directions:

1. Fit the Cuisinart oven with the rack in position 1.
2. Add all ingredients into the mixing bowl and mix until well combined.
3. Make small balls from meat mixture and place onto the parchment-lined baking pan.
4. Set to bake at 425 F for 25 minutes. After 5 minutes place the baking pan in the preheated oven.
5. Serve and enjoy.

Nutritional Value (Amount per Serving):

- Calories 235
- Fat 9.7 g
- Carbohydrates 1.7 g
- Sugar 0.2 g
- Protein 33.6 g
- Cholesterol 143 mg

Delicious Air Fryer Kebabs

Preparation Time: 10 minutes

Cooking Time: 15 minutes

Serve: 4

Ingredients:

- 1 lb ground beef
- 1/4 cup cilantro, chopped
- 1/2 cup onion, minced
- 1/4 tsp ground cinnamon
- 1/2 tsp turmeric
- 1 tbsp ginger garlic paste
- 1/4 tsp ground cardamom
- 1/2 tsp cayenne
- 1 tsp salt

Directions:

1. Fit the Cuisinart oven with the rack in position 2.
2. Add meat and remaining ingredients into the large bowl and mix until well combined.
3. Make sausage shape kebabs and place them in an air fryer basket then place an air fryer basket in the baking pan.
4. Place a baking pan on the oven rack. Set to air fry at 350 F for 15 minutes.
5. Serve and enjoy.

Nutritional Value (Amount per Serving):

- Calories 219
- Fat 7.2 g
- Carbohydrates 1.9 g
- Sugar 0.7 g
- Protein 34.7 g
- Cholesterol 101 mg

Juicy & Tender Pork Chops

Preparation Time: 10 minutes

Cooking Time: 15 minutes

Serve: 4

Ingredients:

- 4 pork chops, boneless
- 1 tsp onion powder
- 1 tsp smoked paprika
- 1/4 cup olive oil
- 1 tsp pepper
- 2 tsp salt

Directions:

1. Fit the Cuisinart oven with the rack in position 1.
2. Brush pork chops with oil and season with onion powder, paprika, pepper, and salt.
3. Place pork chops in a baking pan.
4. Set to bake at 400 F for 20 minutes. After 5 minutes place the baking pan in the preheated oven.
5. Serve and enjoy.

Nutritional Value (Amount per Serving):

- Calories 369
- Fat 32.6 g
- Carbohydrates 1.1 g
- Sugar 0.3 g
- Protein 18.2 g
- Cholesterol 69 mg

Baked Pork Ribs

Preparation Time: 10 minutes

Cooking Time: 30 minutes

Serve: 8

Ingredients:

- 2 lbs pork ribs, boneless
- 1 tbsp onion powder
- 1 1/2 tbsp garlic powder
- Pepper
- Salt

Directions:

1. Fit the Cuisinart oven with the rack in position 1.
2. Place pork ribs in baking pan and season with onion powder, garlic powder, pepper, and salt.
3. Set to bake at 350 F for 35 minutes. After 5 minutes place the baking pan in the preheated oven.
4. Serve and enjoy.

Nutritional Value (Amount per Serving):

- Calories 318
- Fat 20.1 g
- Carbohydrates 1.9 g
- Sugar 0.7 g
- Protein 30.4 g
- Cholesterol 117 mg

Meatballs

Preparation Time: 10 minutes
Cooking Time: 20 minutes
Serve: 4

Ingredients:

- 1 lb ground beef
- 1/2 cup kale, chopped
- 2 garlic cloves, finely chopped
- 1/2 onion, finely chopped
- 4 oz mushrooms, finely chopped
- 3/4 cup cooked quinoa
- 2 tsp Italian seasoning
- 1/4 cup rolled oats
- 1 egg, lightly beaten
- Pepper
- Salt

Directions:

1. Fit the Cuisinart oven with the rack in position 2.
2. Line the air fryer basket with parchment paper.
3. Add all ingredients into a large bowl and mix until well combined.
4. Make small balls from meat mixture and place in the air fryer basket then place the air fryer basket in the baking pan.
5. Place a baking pan on the oven rack. Set to air fry at 380 F for 20 minutes.
6. Serve and enjoy.

Nutritional Value (Amount per Serving):

- Calories 388
- Fat 11.2 g
- Carbohydrates 27.9 g
- Sugar 1.4 g
- Protein 42.4 g
- Cholesterol 144 mg

Flavorful Sirloin Steak

Preparation Time: 10 minutes
Cooking Time: 14 minutes
Serve: 2

Ingredients:

- 1 lb sirloin steaks
- 1/2 tsp garlic powder
- 1/2 tsp onion powder
- 1/4 tsp smoked paprika
- 1 tsp olive oil
- Pepper
- Salt

Directions:

1. Fit the Cuisinart oven with the rack in position 2.
2. Line the air fryer basket with parchment paper.
3. Brush steak with olive oil and rub with garlic powder, onion powder, paprika, pepper, and salt.
4. Place the steak in the air fryer basket then places an air fryer basket in the baking pan.
5. Place a baking pan on the oven rack. Set to air fry at 400 F for 14 minutes.
6. Serve and enjoy.

Nutritional Value (Amount per Serving):

- Calories 447
- Fat 16.5 g
- Carbohydrates 1.2 g
- Sugar 0.4 g
- Protein 69 g
- Cholesterol 203 mg

Tasty Breaded Pork Chops

Preparation Time: 10 minutes

Cooking Time: 12 minutes

Serve: 3

Ingredients:

- 1 egg
- 3 pork chops
- 1/2 cup breadcrumbs
- 1/4 tsp smoked paprika
- 1/2 tsp garlic powder
- 1/2 tsp onion powder
- Pepper
- Salt

Directions:

1. Fit the Cuisinart oven with the rack in position 2.
2. Line the air fryer basket with parchment paper.
3. Season pork chops with paprika, garlic powder, onion powder, pepper, and salt.
4. Place breadcrumbs in a shallow bowl.
5. In a separate shallow bowl, add the egg.
6. Dip pork chop in egg and coat with breadcrumb.
7. Place coated pork chops in the air fryer basket then place an air fryer basket in the baking pan.
8. Place a baking pan on the oven rack. Set to air fry at 380 F for 12 minutes.
9. Serve and enjoy.

Nutritional Value (Amount per Serving):

- Calories 352
- Fat 22.3 g
- Carbohydrates 13.9 g
- Sugar 1.5 g
- Protein 22.4 g
- Cholesterol 123 mg

Air Fryer Juicy Pork Chops

Preparation Time: 10 minutes
Cooking Time: 12 minutes
Serve: 2

Ingredients:
- 2 pork chops
- 2 tbsp brown sugar
- 1 tbsp olive oil
- 1/4 tsp garlic powder
- 1/2 tsp onion powder
- 1 tsp ground mustard
- 1 tbsp paprika
- Pepper
- Salt

Directions:
1. Fit the Cuisinart oven with the rack in position 2.
2. Add all dry ingredients into the small bowl and mix well.
3. Brush pork chops with oil and rub with spice mixture.
4. Place pork chops in the air fryer basket then place an air fryer basket in the baking pan.
5. Place a baking pan on the oven rack. Set to air fry at 400 F for 12 minutes.
6. Serve and enjoy.

Nutritional Value (Amount per Serving):
- Calories 371
- Fat 27.8 g
- Carbohydrates 12.1 g
- Sugar 9.5 g
- Protein 19 g
- Cholesterol 69 mg

Meatballs

Preparation Time: 10 minutes
Cooking Time: 10 minutes
Serve: 4

Ingredients:

- 1 egg, lightly beaten
- 1 lb ground beef
- 1/4 cup onion, chopped
- 2 tbsp taco seasoning
- 1 tbsp garlic, minced
- 1/2 cup cheddar cheese, shredded
- 1/4 cup cilantro, chopped
- Pepper
- Salt

Directions:

1. Fit the Cuisinart oven with the rack in position 2.
2. Line the air fryer basket with parchment paper.
3. Add ground beef and remaining ingredients into the large bowl and mix until well combined.
4. Make small meatballs from meat mixture and place in the air fryer basket then place an air fryer basket in the baking pan.
5. Place a baking pan on the oven rack. Set to air fry at 400 F for 10 minutes.
6. Serve and enjoy.

Nutritional Value (Amount per Serving):

- Calories 290
- Fat 12.9 g
- Carbohydrates 1.7 g
- Sugar 0.5 g
- Protein 39.5 g
- Cholesterol 157 mg

Chapter 5: Fish & Seafood

Italian Cod

Preparation Time: 10 minutes

Cooking Time: 20 minutes

Serve: 4

Ingredients:

- 1 1/2 lbs cod fillet
- 1/4 cup olives, sliced
- 1 lb cherry tomatoes, halved
- 2 garlic cloves, crushed
- 1 small onion, chopped
- 1 tbsp olive oil
- 1/4 cup of water
- 1 tsp Italian seasoning
- Pepper
- Salt

Directions:

1. Fit the Cuisinart oven with the rack in position 1.
2. Place fish fillets, olives, tomatoes, garlic, and onion in a baking dish. Drizzle with oil.
3. Sprinkle with Italian seasoning, pepper, and salt. Pour water into the dish.
4. Set to bake at 400 F for 25 minutes. After 5 minutes place the baking dish in the preheated oven.
5. Serve and enjoy.

Nutritional Value (Amount per Serving):

- Calories 210
- Fat 6.5 g
- Carbohydrates 7.2 g
- Sugar 3.8 g
- Protein 31.7 g
- Cholesterol 84 mg

Paprika Cod

Preparation Time: 10 minutes

Cooking Time: 15 minutes

Serve: 4

Ingredients:

- 4 cod fillets
- 1 tsp smoked paprika
- 1/2 cup parmesan cheese, grated
- 1/2 tbsp olive oil
- 1 tsp parsley
- Pepper
- Salt

Directions:

1. Fit the Cuisinart oven with the rack in position 1.
2. Brush fish fillets with oil and season with pepper and salt.
3. In a shallow dish, mix parmesan cheese, paprika, and parsley.
4. Coat fish fillets with cheese mixture and place into the baking dish.
5. Set to bake at 400 F for 20 minutes. After 5 minutes place the baking dish in the preheated oven.
6. Serve and enjoy.

Nutritional Value (Amount per Serving):

- Calories 125
- Fat 5 g
- Carbohydrates 0.7 g
- Sugar 0.1 g
- Protein 19.8 g
- Cholesterol 52 mg

Tender & Juicy Cajun Cod

Preparation Time: 10 minutes

Cooking Time: 15 minutes

Serve: 6

Ingredients:

- 3 cod fillets, cut in half
- 1 tbsp Cajun seasoning
- 1 tbsp garlic, minced
- 1 tbsp olive oil
- 1/4 cup butter, melted
- Pepper
- Salt

Directions:

1. Fit the Cuisinart oven with the rack in position 1.
2. Season fish fillets with pepper and salt and place in a 9*13-inch baking dish.
3. Mix together the remaining ingredients and pour over fish fillets.
4. Set to bake at 400 F for 20 minutes. After 5 minutes place the baking dish in the preheated oven.
5. Serve and enjoy.

Nutritional Value (Amount per Serving):

- Calories 126
- Fat 10.4 g
- Carbohydrates 0.5 g
- Sugar 0 g
- Protein 8.2 g
- Cholesterol 42 mg

Easy Baked Fish Fillet

Preparation Time: 10 minutes

Cooking Time: 15 minutes

Serve: 4

Ingredients:

- 1 lb white fish fillets
- 2 tbsp dried parsley
- 1/4 tsp red chili flakes
- 2 tbsp garlic, minced
- 2 tbsp olive oil
- Pepper
- Salt

Directions:

1. Fit the Cuisinart oven with the rack in position 1.
2. Place fish fillets in a baking dish and drizzle with oil.
3. Sprinkle with chili flakes, parsley, and garlic. Season with pepper and salt.
4. Set to bake at 400 F for 20 minutes. After 5 minutes place the baking dish in the preheated oven.
5. Serve and enjoy.

Nutritional Value (Amount per Serving):

- Calories 262
- Fat 15.6 g
- Carbohydrates 1.5 g
- Sugar 0.1 g
- Protein 28.1 g
- Cholesterol 87 mg

Perfect Crab Cakes

Preparation Time: 10 minutes
Cooking Time: 30 minutes
Serve: 6

Ingredients:
- 16 oz lump crab meat
- 1/4 cup celery, diced
- 1/4 cup onion, diced
- 1 cup crushed crackers
- 1 tsp old bay seasoning
- 1 tsp brown mustard
- 2/3 cup mashed avocado

Directions:
1. Fit the Cuisinart oven with the rack in position 1.
2. Add all ingredients into the bowl and mix until just combined.
3. Make small patties from mixture and place in parchment-lined baking pan.
4. Set to bake at 350 F for 35 minutes. After 5 minutes place the baking dish in the preheated oven.
5. Serve and enjoy.

Nutritional Value (Amount per Serving):
- Calories 84
- Fat 7.7 g
- Carbohydrates 4.6 g
- Sugar 0.8 g
- Protein 11.5 g
- Cholesterol 43 mg

Old Bay Seasoned Scallops

Preparation Time: 10 minutes

Cooking Time: 4 minutes

Serve: 4

Ingredients:

- 1 lb sea scallops
- 1/2 tsp garlic powder
- 1/2 cup crushed crackers
- 2 tbsp butter, melted
- 1/2 tsp old bay seasoning

Directions:

1. Fit the Cuisinart oven with the rack in position 2.
2. In a shallow dish, mix crushed crackers, garlic powder, and old bay seasoning.
3. Add melted butter in a separate shallow dish.
4. Dip scallops in melted butter and coat with crushed crackers.
5. Place coated scallops in air fryer basket then place air fryer basket in baking pan.
6. Place a baking pan on the oven rack. Set to air fry at 390 F for 4 minutes.
7. Serve and enjoy.

Nutritional Value (Amount per Serving):

- Calories 167
- Fat 7.4 g
- Carbohydrates 4.8 g
- Sugar 0.5 g
- Protein 19.5 g
- Cholesterol 53 mg

Cajun Red Snapper

Preparation Time: 10 minutes

Cooking Time: 12 minutes

Serve: 2

Ingredients:

- 8 oz red snapper fillets
- 2 tbsp parmesan cheese, grated
- 1/4 cup breadcrumbs
- 1/2 tsp Cajun seasoning
- 1/4 tsp Worcestershire sauce
- 1 garlic clove, minced
- 1/4 cup butter

Directions:

1. Fit the Cuisinart oven with the rack in position 1.
2. Melt butter in a pan over low heat. Add Cajun seasoning, garlic, and Worcestershire sauce into the melted butter and stir well.
3. Brush fish fillets with melted butter and place into the baking dish.
4. Mix together parmesan cheese and breadcrumbs and sprinkle over fish fillets.
5. Set to bake at 400 F for 17 minutes. After 5 minutes place the baking dish in the preheated oven.
6. Serve and enjoy.

Nutritional Value (Amount per Serving):

- Calories 424
- Fat 27 g
- Carbohydrates 10.6 g
- Sugar 1 g
- Protein 33.9 g
- Cholesterol 119 mg

Flavorful Baked Halibut

Preparation Time: 10 minutes
Cooking Time: 12 minutes
Serve: 4

Ingredients:
- 1 lb halibut fillets
- 1/4 tsp garlic powder
- 1/4 tsp paprika
- 1/4 tsp smoked paprika
- 1/4 tsp pepper
- 1/4 cup olive oil
- 1 lemon juice
- 1/2 tsp salt

Directions:
1. Fit the Cuisinart oven with the rack in position 1.
2. Place fish fillets into the baking dish.
3. In a small bowl, mix lemon juice, oil, paprika, smoked paprika, garlic powder, and salt.
4. Brush lemon juice mixture over fish fillets.
5. Set to bake at 425 F for 17 minutes. After 5 minutes place the baking dish in the preheated oven.
6. Serve and enjoy.

Nutritional Value (Amount per Serving):
- Calories 236
- Fat 15.3 g
- Carbohydrates 0.4 g
- Sugar 0.1 g
- Protein 24 g
- Cholesterol 36 mg

Lemon Butter Shrimp

Preparation Time: 10 minutes

Cooking Time: 12 minutes

Serve: 4

Ingredients:

- 1 1/4 lbs shrimp, peeled & deveined
- 2 tbsp fresh parsley, chopped
- 2 tbsp fresh lemon juice
- 1 tbsp garlic, minced
- 1/4 cup butter
- Pepper
- Salt

Directions:

1. Fit the Cuisinart oven with the rack in position 1.
2. Add shrimp into the baking dish.
3. Melt butter in a pan over low heat. Add garlic and sauté for 30 seconds. Stir in lemon juice.
4. Pour melted butter mixture over shrimp. Season with pepper and salt.
5. Set to bake at 350 F for 17 minutes. After 5 minutes place the baking dish in the preheated oven.
6. Garnish with parsley and serve.

Nutritional Value (Amount per Serving):

- Calories 276
- Fat 14 g
- Carbohydrates 3.2 g
- Sugar 0.2 g
- Protein 32.7 g
- Cholesterol 329 mg

Baked Buttery Shrimp

Preparation Time: 10 minutes

Cooking Time: 15 minutes

Serve: 4

Ingredients:

- 1 lb shrimp, peel & deveined
- 2 tsp garlic powder
- 2 tsp dry mustard
- 2 tsp cumin
- 2 tsp paprika
- 2 tsp black pepper
- 4 tsp cayenne pepper
- 1/2 cup butter, melted
- 2 tsp onion powder
- 1 tsp dried oregano
- 1 tsp dried thyme
- 3 tsp salt

Directions:

1. Fit the Cuisinart oven with the rack in position 1.
2. Add shrimp, butter, and remaining ingredients into the mixing bowl and toss well.
3. Transfer shrimp mixture into the baking pan.
4. Set to bake at 400 F for 20 minutes. After 5 minutes place the baking pan in the preheated oven.
5. Serve and enjoy.

Nutritional Value (Amount per Serving):

- Calories 372
- Fat 26.2 g
- Carbohydrates 7.5 g
- Sugar 1.3 g
- Protein 27.6 g
- Cholesterol 300 mg

Dijon Salmon Fillets

Preparation Time: 10 minutes
Cooking Time: 15 minutes
Serve: 4

Ingredients:

- 1 lb salmon fillets
- 2 tbsp Dijon mustard
- 1/4 cup brown sugar
- Pepper
- Salt

Directions:

1. Fit the Cuisinart oven with the rack in position 2.
2. Season salmon fillets with pepper and salt.
3. In a small bowl, mix Dijon mustard and brown sugar.
4. Brush salmon fillets with Dijon mustard mixture.
5. Place salmon fillets in the air fryer basket then place an air fryer basket in the baking pan.
6. Place a baking pan on the oven rack. Set to air fry at 350 F for 15 minutes.
7. Serve and enjoy.

Nutritional Value (Amount per Serving):

- Calories 190
- Fat 7.3 g
- Carbohydrates 9.3 g
- Sugar 8.9 g
- Protein 22.4 g
- Cholesterol 50 mg

Delicious Crab Cakes

Preparation Time: 10 minutes

Cooking Time: 10 minutes

Serve: 5

Ingredients:

- 18 oz can crab meat, drained
- 2 1/2 tbsp mayonnaise
- 2 eggs, lightly beaten
- 1/4 cup breadcrumbs
- 1 1/2 tsp dried parsley
- 1 tbsp dried celery
- 1 tsp Old bay seasoning
- 1 1/2 tbsp Dijon mustard
- Pepper
- Salt

Directions:

1. Fit the Cuisinart oven with the rack in position 2.
2. Add all ingredients into the mixing bowl and mix until well combined.
3. Make patties from mixture and place in the air fryer basket then place an air fryer basket in the baking pan.
4. Place a baking pan on the oven rack. Set to air fry at 320 F for 10 minutes.
5. Serve and enjoy.

Nutritional Value (Amount per Serving):

- Calories 138
- Fat 4.7 g
- Carbohydrates 7.8 g
- Sugar 2.7 g
- Protein 16.8 g
- Cholesterol 127 mg

Miso White Fish Fillets

Preparation Time: 10 minutes
Cooking Time: 10 minutes
Serve: 2

Ingredients:

- 2 cod fish fillets
- 2 tbsp brown sugar
- 2 tbsp miso
- 1 tbsp garlic, chopped

Directions:

1. Fit the Cuisinart oven with the rack in position 2.
2. Add all ingredients to the zip-lock bag and marinate fish in the refrigerator overnight.
3. Place marinated fish fillets in the air fryer basket then place an air fryer basket in the baking pan.
4. Place a baking pan on the oven rack. Set to air fry at 350 F for 10 minutes.
5. Serve and enjoy.

Nutritional Value (Amount per Serving):

- Calories 9
- Fat 0.1 g
- Carbohydrates 0.5 g
- Sugar 0.3 g
- Protein 1.5 g
- Cholesterol 3 mg

Spinach Scallops

Preparation Time: 10 minutes
Cooking Time: 10 minutes
Serve: 2

Ingredients:

- 8 sea scallops
- 1 tbsp fresh basil, chopped
- 1 tbsp tomato paste
- 3/4 cup heavy cream
- 12 oz frozen spinach, thawed and drained
- 1 tsp garlic, minced
- 1/2 tsp pepper
- 1/2 tsp salt

Directions:

1. Fit the Cuisinart oven with the rack in position 1.
2. Layer spinach in the baking dish.
3. Spray scallops with cooking spray and season with pepper and salt.
4. Place scallops on top of spinach.
5. In a small bowl, mix garlic, basil, tomato paste, whipping cream, pepper, and salt and pour over scallops and spinach.
6. Set to bake at 350 F for 15 minutes. After 5 minutes place the baking dish in the preheated oven.
7. Serve and enjoy.

Nutritional Value (Amount per Serving):

- Calories 310
- Fat 18.3 g
- Carbohydrates 12.6 g
- Sugar 1.7 g
- Protein 26.5 g
- Cholesterol 101 mg

Basil Tomato Salmon

Preparation Time: 10 minutes

Cooking Time: 20 minutes

Serve: 2

Ingredients:

- 2 salmon fillets
- 1 tomato, sliced
- 1 tbsp dried basil
- 2 tbsp parmesan cheese, grated
- 1 tbsp olive oil

Directions:

1. Fit the Cuisinart oven with the rack in position 1.
2. Place salmon fillets in a baking dish.
3. Sprinkle basil on top of salmon fillets.
4. Arrange tomato slices on top of salmon fillets. Drizzle with oil and top with cheese.
5. Set to bake at 375 F for 25 minutes. After 5 minutes place the baking dish in the preheated oven.
6. Serve and enjoy.

Nutritional Value (Amount per Serving):

- Calories 324
- Fat 19.6 g
- Carbohydrates 1.5 g
- Sugar 0.8 g
- Protein 37.1 g
- Cholesterol 83 mg

Chapter 6: Vegetables & Side Dishes

Cheese Herb Zucchini

Preparation Time: 10 minutes
Cooking Time: 15 minutes
Serve: 4

Ingredients:

- 4 zucchini, quartered
- 1/2 tsp dried oregano
- 2 tbsp fresh parsley, chopped
- 2 tbsp olive oil
- 1/2 tsp dried thyme
- 1/2 cup parmesan cheese, grated
- 1/4 tsp garlic powder
- 1/2 tsp dried basil
- Pepper
- Salt

Directions:

1. Fit the Cuisinart oven with the rack in position 1.
2. In a small bowl, mix parmesan cheese, garlic powder, basil, oregano, thyme, pepper, and salt.
3. Arrange zucchini in baking pan and drizzle with oil and sprinkle with parmesan cheese mixture.
4. Set to bake at 350 F for 20 minutes. After 5 minutes place the baking pan in the preheated oven.
5. Garnish with parsley and serve.

Nutritional Value (Amount per Serving):

- Calories 130
- Fat 9.8 g
- Carbohydrates 7.4 g
- Sugar 3.5 g
- Protein 6.1 g
- Cholesterol 8 mg

Healthy Barley Bread

Preparation Time: 10 minutes

Cooking Time: 40 minutes

Serve: 16

Ingredients:
- 2 eggs
- 1/2 tsp baking soda
- 2 tbsp baking powder
- 3 cups barley flour
- 3 tbsp honey
- 1/3 cup olive oil
- 1 1/2 cups buttermilk
- 1 1/4 tsp salt

Directions:
1. Fit the Cuisinart oven with the rack in position 1.
2. In a large bowl, mix together flour, baking powder, baking soda, and salt.
3. In a separate bowl, whisk eggs with honey, oil, and buttermilk.
4. Add egg mixture into the flour mixture and stir until just combined.
5. Pour batter into the greased loaf pan.
6. Set to bake at 350 F for 40 minutes. After 5 minutes place the loaf pan in the preheated oven.
7. Slice and serve.

Nutritional Value (Amount per Serving):
- Calories 163
- Fat 5.4 g
- Carbohydrates 26 g
- Sugar 4.6 g
- Protein 4.4 g
- Cholesterol 21 mg

Baked Vegetables

Preparation Time: 10 minutes
Cooking Time: 30 minutes
Serve: 6

Ingredients:

- 2 zucchini, sliced
- 2 tomatoes, quartered
- 6 fresh basil leaves, sliced
- 2 tsp Italian seasoning
- 2 tbsp olive oil
- 1 eggplant, sliced
- 1 onion, sliced
- 1 bell pepper, cut into strips
- Pepper
- Salt

Directions:

1. Fit the Cuisinart oven with the rack in position 1.
2. Add all ingredients except basil leaves into the bowl and toss well.
3. Transfer vegetable mixture in parchment-lined baking pan.
4. Set to bake at 400 F for 35 minutes. After 5 minutes place the baking pan in the preheated oven.
5. Garnish with basil and serve.

Nutritional Value (Amount per Serving):

- Calories 96
- Fat 5.5 g
- Carbohydrates 11.7 g
- Sugar 6.4 g
- Protein 2.3 g
- Cholesterol 1 mg

Cheesy Broccoli Rice

Preparation Time: 10 minutes

Cooking Time: 20 minutes

Serve: 8

Ingredients:

- 1 1/2 cups cooked brown rice
- 1 garlic clove, chopped
- 16 oz frozen broccoli florets
- 1 large onion, chopped
- 1 tbsp butter
- 3 tbsp parmesan cheese, grated
- 10.5 oz condensed cheddar cheese soup
- 1/3 cup almond milk

Directions:

1. Fit the Cuisinart oven with the rack in position 1.
2. Heat butter in a 10-inch pan over medium heat.
3. Add onion and cook until tender.
4. Add garlic and broccoli in the pan and cook until broccoli is tender.
5. Stir in rice, soup, and milk and cook until hot.
6. Stir in cheese and pour broccoli mixture into the greased baking dish.
7. Set to bake at 350 F for 25 minutes. After 5 minutes place the baking dish in the preheated oven.
8. Serve and enjoy.

Nutritional Value (Amount per Serving):

- Calories 244
- Fat 8.3 g
- Carbohydrates 35.4 g
- Sugar 2.7 g
- Protein 6 g
- Cholesterol 14 mg

Baked Cauliflower & Mushrooms

Preparation Time: 10 minutes

Cooking Time: 20 minutes

Serve: 6

Ingredients:

- 1 lb mushrooms, cleaned
- 8 garlic cloves, peeled
- 2 cups cherry tomatoes
- 2 cups cauliflower florets
- 1 tbsp fresh parsley, chopped
- 1 tbsp Italian seasoning
- 2 tbsp olive oil
- Pepper
- Salt

Directions:

1. Fit the Cuisinart oven with the rack in position 1.
2. Add cauliflower, mushrooms, Italian seasoning, olive oil, garlic, cherry tomatoes, pepper, and salt into the mixing bowl and toss well.
3. Transfer cauliflower and mushroom mixture on a baking pan.
4. Set to bake at 400 F for 25 minutes. After 5 minutes place the baking pan in the preheated oven.
5. Garnish with parsley and serve.

Nutritional Value (Amount per Serving):

- Calories 89
- Fat 5.8 g
- Carbohydrates 8.2 g
- Sugar 3.9 g
- Protein 3.8 g
- Cholesterol 2 mg

Jalapeno Bread

Preparation Time: 10 minutes
Cooking Time: 50 minutes
Serve: 10

Ingredients:
- 3 cups all-purpose flour
- 8 oz cheddar cheese, shredded
- 1/2 tsp ground white pepper
- 1 1/2 tbsp baking powder
- 1/4 cup butter, melted
- 1 1/2 cups buttermilk
- 3 jalapeno peppers, chopped
- 2 tbsp sugar
- 1 1/4 tsp salt

Directions:
1. Fit the Cuisinart oven with the rack in position 1.
2. In a mixing bowl, mix flour, baking powder, sugar, white pepper, and salt.
3. Add jalapenos and cheese and stir to combine.
4. Whisk butter and buttermilk together and add to the flour mixture. Stir until just combined.
5. Pour batter into the greased 9*5-inch loaf pan.
6. Set to bake at 375 F for 55 minutes. After 5 minutes place the loaf pan in the preheated oven.
7. Slice and serve.

Nutritional Value (Amount per Serving):
- Calories 297
- Fat 12.9 g
- Carbohydrates 34.5 g
- Sugar 4.5 g
- Protein 10.9 g
- Cholesterol 37 mg

Honey Corn Muffins

Preparation Time: 10 minutes

Cooking Time: 20 minutes

Serve: 8

Ingredients:

- 2 eggs
- 1/2 cup sugar
- 1 1/4 cups self-rising flour
- 3/4 cup yellow cornmeal
- 1/2 cup butter, melted
- 3/4 cup buttermilk
- 1 tbsp honey

Directions:

1. Fit the Cuisinart oven with the rack in position 1.
2. Spray 8-cups muffin tin with cooking spray and set aside.
3. In a large bowl, mix together cornmeal, sugar, and flour.
4. In a separate bowl, whisk the eggs with buttermilk and honey until well combined.
5. Slowly add egg mixture and melted butter to the cornmeal mixture and stir until just mixed.
6. Spoon batter into the prepared muffin tin.
7. Set to bake at 350 F for 25 minutes. After 5 minutes place muffin tin in the preheated oven.
8. Serve and enjoy.

Nutritional Value (Amount per Serving):

- Calories 294
- Fat 13.4 g
- Carbohydrates 39.6 g
- Sugar 16 g
- Protein 5.2 g
- Cholesterol 72 mg

Tasty Butternut Squash

Preparation Time: 10 minutes

Cooking Time: 15 minutes

Serve: 4

Ingredients:

- 4 cups butternut squash, cut into 1-inch pieces
- 1 tbsp brown sugar
- 2 tbsp olive oil
- 1 tsp Chinese 5 spice powder

Directions:

1. Fit the Cuisinart oven with the rack in position 2.
2. Toss squash into the bowl with remaining ingredients.
3. Transfer squash in the air fryer basket then places the air fryer basket in the baking pan.
4. Place a baking pan on the oven rack. Set to air fry at 400 F for 15 minutes.
5. Serve and enjoy.

Nutritional Value (Amount per Serving):

- Calories 132
- Fat 7.1 g
- Carbohydrates 18.6 g
- Sugar 5.3 g
- Protein 1.4 g
- Cholesterol 0 mg

Brussels Sprouts & Sweet Potatoes

Preparation Time: 10 minutes

Cooking Time: 15 minutes

Serve: 6

Ingredients:

- 1 lb sweet potatoes, peeled and diced into 1/2-inch cubes
- 1 lb Brussels sprouts, remove stem & into quartered
- 2 tbsp olive oil
- 1 tsp chili powder
- Pepper
- Salt

Directions:

1. Fit the Cuisinart oven with the rack in position 2.
2. Add Brussels sprouts, sweet potatoes, chili powder, olive oil, pepper, and salt into the mixing bowl and toss well.
3. Transfer Brussels sprouts & sweet potato mixture in air fryer basket then place air fryer basket in baking pan.
4. Place a baking pan on the oven rack. Set to air fry at 380 F for 15 minutes.
5. Serve and enjoy.

Nutritional Value (Amount per Serving):

- Calories 163
- Fat 5.1 g
- Carbohydrates 28.2 g
- Sugar 2 g
- Protein 3.8 g
- Cholesterol 0 mg

Parmesan Baked Asparagus

Preparation Time: 10 minutes

Cooking Time: 12 minutes

Serve: 4

Ingredients:
- 1 lb asparagus, wash, trimmed, and cut the ends
- 1 tbsp dried parsley
- 2 garlic cloves, minced
- 2 tbsp olive oil
- 3 oz parmesan cheese, shaved
- 1 tsp dried oregano
- Pepper
- Salt

Directions:
1. Fit the Cuisinart oven with the rack in position 1.
2. Arrange asparagus in baking pan. Drizzle with olive oil and season with pepper and salt.
3. Spread cheese, oregano, parsley, and garlic over the asparagus
4. Set to bake at 425 F for 17 minutes. After 5 minutes place the baking pan in the preheated oven.
5. Serve and enjoy.

Nutritional Value (Amount per Serving):
- Calories 155
- Fat 11.8 g
- Carbohydrates 6 g
- Sugar 2.2 g
- Protein 9.5 g
- Cholesterol 15 mg

Chili Lime Sweet Potatoes

Preparation Time: 10 minutes

Cooking Time: 15 minutes

Serve: 4

Ingredients:

- 2 large sweet potatoes, peeled & cut into 1-inch pieces
- 1 tbsp chili powder
- 2 tbsp olive oil
- 2 tsp fresh lime juice
- 1 tsp cumin

Directions:

1. Fit the Cuisinart oven with the rack in position 2.
2. In a mixing bowl, add sweet potatoes, lime juice, cumin, chili powder, and olive oil and toss well.
3. Transfer sweet potatoes in air fryer basket then place air fryer basket in baking pan.
4. Place a baking pan on the oven rack. Set to air fry at 380 F for 20 minutes.
5. Serve and enjoy.

Nutritional Value (Amount per Serving):

- Calories 132
- Fat 1.1 g
- Carbohydrates 17.1 g
- Sugar 0.8 g
- Protein 1.2 g
- Cholesterol 0 mg

Baked Potatoes Eggplant

Preparation Time: 10 minutes

Cooking Time: 40 minutes

Serve: 4

Ingredients:

- 2 medium eggplants, cut into pieces
- 1 tbsp lemon juice
- 1 lb potatoes, cut into cubes
- 1/4 cup olive oil
- Pepper
- Salt

Directions:

1. Fit the Cuisinart oven with the rack in position 1.
2. Add eggplant, potatoes, oil, pepper, and salt in a baking dish and toss well.
3. Set to bake at 400 F for 45 minutes. After 5 minutes place the baking dish in the preheated oven.
4. Drizzle with lemon juice and serve.

Nutritional Value (Amount per Serving):

- Calories 244
- Fat 13.2 g
- Carbohydrates 31.4 g
- Sugar 8.3 g
- Protein 4.2 g
- Cholesterol 0 mg

Tasty Hassel Back Potatoes

Preparation Time: 10 minutes
Cooking Time: 30 minutes
Serve: 4

Ingredients:

- 4 potatoes, peel & cut potato across the potato to make 1/8-inch slices
- 1/4 cup parmesan cheese, shredded
- 1 tbsp olive oil

Directions:

1. Fit the Cuisinart oven with the rack in position 2.
2. Brush potatoes with olive oil.
3. Place potatoes in the air fryer basket then place an air fryer basket in the baking pan.
4. Place a baking pan on the oven rack. Set to air fry at 350 F for 30 minutes.
5. Sprinkle cheese on top of potatoes and serve.

Nutritional Value (Amount per Serving):

- Calories 195
- Fat 4.9 g
- Carbohydrates 33.7 g
- Sugar 2.5 g
- Protein 5.4 g
- Cholesterol 4 mg

Air Fried Eggplant Cubes

Preparation Time: 10 minutes

Cooking Time: 12 minutes

Serve: 2

Ingredients:

- 1 eggplant, cut into cubes
- 1/4 tsp oregano
- 1 tbsp olive oil
- 1/2 tsp garlic powder

Directions:

1. Fit the Cuisinart oven with the rack in position 2.
2. Add all ingredients into the large bowl and toss well.
3. Transfer eggplant into in air fryer basket then places the air fryer basket in the baking pan.
4. Place a baking pan on the oven rack. Set to air fry at 390 F for 12 minutes.
5. Serve and enjoy.

Nutritional Value (Amount per Serving):

- Calories 120
- Fat 7.4 g
- Carbohydrates 14.1 g
- Sugar 7.1 g
- Protein 2.4 g
- Cholesterol 0 mg

Lemon Garlic Brussels Sprouts

Preparation Time: 10 minutes

Cooking Time: 12 minutes

Serve: 2

Ingredients:

- 1/2 lb Brussels sprouts, rinse and pat dry with a paper towel
- 1/2 tsp garlic powder
- 1 tbsp lemon juice
- 1/4 tsp black pepper
- 1 tbsp olive oil
- 1/2 tsp salt

Directions:

1. Fit the Cuisinart oven with the rack in position 2.
2. Cut the stem of Brussels sprouts and cut each Brussels sprouts in half.
3. Transfer Brussels sprouts in a bowl and toss with garlic powder, olive oil, pepper, and salt.
4. Transfer Brussels sprouts in air fryer basket then place air fryer basket in baking pan.
5. Place baking pan on the oven rack. Set to air fry at 360 F for 12 minutes.
6. Drizzle with lemon juice and serve.

Nutritional Value (Amount per Serving):

- Calories 114
- Fat 7.5 g
- Carbohydrates 11.2 g
- Sugar 2.8 g
- Protein 4.1 g
- Cholesterol 0 mg

Chapter 7: Snacks & Appetizers

Cheesy Onion Dip

Preparation Time: 10 minutes

Cooking Time: 40 minutes

Serve: 8

Ingredients:

- 1 1/2 onions, chopped
- 1/2 tsp garlic powder
- 1 1/2 cup Swiss cheese, shredded
- 1 cup mozzarella cheese, shredded
- 1 cup cheddar cheese, shredded
- 1 1/2 cup mayonnaise
- Pepper
- Salt

Directions:

1. Fit the Cuisinart oven with the rack in position 1.
2. Add all ingredients into the mixing bowl and mix until well combined.
3. Pour mixture into the prepared baking dish.
4. Set to bake at 350 F for 45 minutes. After 5 minutes place the baking dish in the preheated oven.
5. Serve and enjoy.

Nutritional Value (Amount per Serving):

- Calories 325
- Fat 25.7 g
- Carbohydrates 14 g
- Sugar 4.1 g
- Protein 10.6 g
- Cholesterol 47 mg

Air Fryer Walnuts

Preparation Time: 10 minutes

Cooking Time: 5 minutes

Serve: 6

Ingredients:

- 2 cups walnuts
- 1 tsp olive oil
- Pepper
- Salt

Directions:

1. Fit the Cuisinart oven with the rack in position 2.
2. Add walnuts, oil, pepper, and salt into the bowl and toss well.
3. Add walnuts to the air fryer basket then place an air fryer basket in baking pan.
4. Place a baking pan on the oven rack. Set to air fry at 350 F for 5 minutes.
5. Serve and enjoy.

Nutritional Value (Amount per Serving):

- Calories 264
- Fat 25.4 g
- Carbohydrates 4.1 g
- Sugar 0.5 g
- Protein 10 g
- Cholesterol 0 mg

Spicy Brussels Sprouts

Preparation Time: 10 minutes

Cooking Time: 35 minutes

Serve: 6

Ingredients:
- 2 cups Brussels sprouts, halved
- 1/4 tsp cayenne pepper
- 1/2 tsp smoked paprika
- 1/4 tsp chili powder
- 1/4 tsp garlic powder
- 1/4 cup olive oil
- 1/4 tsp salt

Directions:
1. Fit the Cuisinart oven with the rack in position 1.
2. Add all ingredients into the large bowl and toss well.
3. Transfer Brussels sprouts on a baking pan.
4. Set to bake at 400 F for 40 minutes. After 5 minutes place the baking pan in the preheated oven.
5. Serve and enjoy.

Nutritional Value (Amount per Serving):
- Calories 86
- Fat 8.6 g
- Carbohydrates 3 g
- Sugar 0.7 g
- Protein 1.1 g
- Cholesterol 0 mg

Jalapeno Spinach Dip

Preparation Time: 10 minutes

Cooking Time: 30 minutes

Serve: 6

Ingredients:

- 10 oz frozen spinach, thawed and drained
- 2 tsp jalapeno pepper, minced
- 1/2 cup cheddar cheese, shredded
- 8 oz cream cheese
- 1/2 cup onion, diced
- 2 tsp garlic, minced
- 1/2 cup mozzarella cheese, shredded
- 1/2 cup Monterey jack cheese, shredded
- 1/2 tsp salt

Directions:

1. Fit the Cuisinart oven with the rack in position 1.
2. Add all ingredients into the mixing bowl and mix until well combined.
3. Pour mixture into the 1-quart casserole dish.
4. Set to bake at 350 F for 35 minutes. After 5 minutes place the casserole dish in the preheated oven.
5. Serve and enjoy.

Nutritional Value (Amount per Serving):

- Calories 228
- Fat 19.8 g
- Carbohydrates 4.2 g
- Sugar 0.8 g
- Protein 9.7 g
- Cholesterol 61 mg

Tasty Sweet Potato Fries

Preparation Time: 10 minutes

Cooking Time: 20 minutes

Serve: 2

Ingredients:

- 2 small sweet potatoes, peel and cut into fries shape
- 2 tbsp olive oil
- 1/4 tsp sea salt
- 1/4 tsp coriander
- 1/2 tsp curry powder

Directions:

1. Fit the Cuisinart oven with the rack in position 2.
2. Add all ingredients into the large mixing bowl and toss well.
3. Spray air fryer basket with cooking spray.
4. Transfer sweet potato fries in the air fryer basket then place the air fryer basket in the baking pan.
5. Place a baking pan on the oven rack. Set to air fry at 370 F for 20 minutes.
6. Serve and enjoy.

Nutritional Value (Amount per Serving):

- Calories 240
- Fat 14.2 g
- Carbohydrates 28.3 g
- Sugar 0.5 g
- Protein 1.6 g
- Cholesterol 0 mg

Habanero Chicken Wings

Preparation Time: 10 minutes

Cooking Time: 16 minutes

Serve: 6

Ingredients:

- 1 1/2 lbs chicken wings
- 2 tbsp habanero hot sauce
- 2 garlic cloves, chopped
- 1 tsp pepper
- 1 tsp garlic salt
- 1 tsp cayenne pepper
- 1/2 tbsp soy sauce

Directions:

1. Fit the Cuisinart oven with the rack in position 2.
2. Add chicken wings into the large bowl and toss with remaining ingredients.
3. Transfer chicken wings in air fryer basket then place air fryer basket in baking pan.
4. Place a baking pan on the oven rack. Set to air fry at 360 F for 16 minutes.
5. Serve and enjoy.

Nutritional Value (Amount per Serving):

- Calories 226
- Fat 8.5 g
- Carbohydrates 2.2 g
- Sugar 0.2 g
- Protein 33.1 g
- Cholesterol 101 mg

Air Fryer Radish Chips

Preparation Time: 10 minutes

Cooking Time: 15 minutes

Serve: 12

Ingredients:

- 1 lb radish, wash and slice into chips
- 1/4 tsp pepper
- 2 tbsp olive oil
- 1 tsp salt

Directions:

1. Fit the Cuisinart oven with the rack in position 2.
2. Add all ingredients into the large bowl and toss well.
3. Add radish slices to the air fryer basket then place an air fryer basket in baking pan.
4. Place a baking pan on the oven rack. Set to air fry at 375 F for 15 minutes.
5. Serve and enjoy.

Nutritional Value (Amount per Serving):

- Calories 26
- Fat 2.4 g
- Carbohydrates 1.3 g
- Sugar 0.7 g
- Protein 0.3 g
- Cholesterol 0 mg

Delicious Jalapeno Poppers

Preparation Time: 10 minutes

Cooking Time: 7 minutes

Serve: 10

Ingredients:

- 10 jalapeno peppers, cut in half, remove seeds & membranes
- 1/2 cup cheddar cheese, shredded
- 4 oz cream cheese
- 1/4 tsp paprika
- 1 tsp ground cumin
- 1 tsp salt

Directions:

1. Fit the Cuisinart oven with the rack in position 2.
2. In a small bowl, mix together cream cheese, cheddar cheese, cumin, paprika, and salt.
3. Stuff cream cheese mixture into each jalapeno half.
4. Place stuffed jalapeno peppers in air fryer basket then place air fryer basket in baking pan.
5. Place a baking pan on the oven rack. Set to air fry at 350 F for 7 minutes.
6. Serve and enjoy.

Nutritional Value (Amount per Serving):

- Calories 69
- Fat 6.1 g
- Carbohydrates 1.5 g
- Sugar 0.5 g
- Protein 2.5 g
- Cholesterol 18 mg

Air Fryer Cabbage Chips

Preparation Time: 10 minutes

Cooking Time: 25 minutes

Serve: 6

Ingredients:

- 1 large cabbage head, tear cabbage leaves into pieces
- 2 tbsp olive oil
- 1/4 cup parmesan cheese, grated
- Pepper
- Salt

Directions:

1. Fit the Cuisinart oven with the rack in position 2.
2. Add all ingredients into the large mixing bowl and toss well.
3. Add cabbage pieces to the air fryer basket then place an air fryer basket in the baking pan.
4. Place a baking pan on the oven rack. Set to air fry at 300 F for 25 minutes.
5. Serve and enjoy.

Nutritional Value (Amount per Serving):

- Calories 104
- Fat 5.7 g
- Carbohydrates 12.2 g
- Sugar 6.7 g
- Protein 3.9 g
- Cholesterol 3 mg

Cheesy Brussels Sprouts

Preparation Time: 10 minutes
Cooking Time: 12 minutes
Serve: 4

Ingredients:
- 1 lb Brussels sprouts, cut stems and halved
- 1/4 cup parmesan cheese, grated
- 1 tbsp olive oil
- 1/4 tsp paprika
- 1/4 tsp chili powder
- 1/2 tsp garlic powder
- Pepper
- Salt

Directions:
1. Fit the Cuisinart oven with the rack in position 2.
2. Toss Brussels sprouts with remaining ingredients except for cheese and place in air fryer basket then place air fryer basket in baking pan.
3. Place a baking pan on the oven rack. Set to air fry at 350 F for 12 minutes.
4. Top with parmesan cheese and serve.

Nutritional Value (Amount per Serving):
- Calories 100
- Fat 5.2 g
- Carbohydrates 11 g
- Sugar 2.6 g
- Protein 5.8 g
- Cholesterol 4 mg

Zucchini Coconut Bites

Preparation Time: 10 minutes
Cooking Time: 10 minutes
Serve: 6

Ingredients:
- 4 zucchini, grated and squeeze out all liquid
- 1 cup shredded coconut
- 1 egg, lightly beaten
- 1 tsp Italian seasoning
- 1/2 cup parmesan cheese, grated

Directions:
1. Fit the Cuisinart oven with the rack in position 2.
2. Add all ingredients into the bowl and mix until well combined.
3. Make small balls from the zucchini mixture and place in the air fryer basket then place the air fryer basket in the baking pan.
4. Place a baking pan on the oven rack. Set to air fry at 400 F for 10 minutes.
5. Serve and enjoy.

Nutritional Value (Amount per Serving):
- Calories 105
- Fat 7.3 g
- Carbohydrates 6.8 g
- Sugar 3.2 g
- Protein 5.4 g
- Cholesterol 33 mg

Yummy Turkey Jalapeno Poppers

Preparation Time: 10 minutes
Cooking Time: 20 minutes
Serve: 12

Ingredients:

- 1/2 cup turkey, cooked and shredded
- 4 oz cream cheese
- 1/4 tsp dried basil
- 6 jalapenos, halved and seed removed
- 1/4 cup mozzarella cheese, shredded
- 1/4 tsp salt

Directions:

1. Fit the Cuisinart oven with the rack in position 2.
2. Mix all ingredients in a bowl except jalapenos.
3. Stuff cheese mixture into each jalapeno half and place in the air fryer basket then place the air fryer basket in the baking pan.
4. Place a baking pan on the oven rack. Set to air fry at 370 F for 20 minutes.
5. Serve and enjoy.

Nutritional Value (Amount per Serving):

- Calories 54
- Fat 4.2 g
- Carbohydrates 0.9 g
- Sugar 0.3 g
- Protein 3.1 g
- Cholesterol 17 mg

Air Fryer Nuts

Preparation Time: 10 minutes

Cooking Time: 9 minutes

Serve: 4

Ingredients:

- 1/2 cup macadamia nuts
- 1/4 cup walnuts
- 1/4 cup hazelnuts
- 1/2 cup pecans
- 1 tbsp olive oil
- 1 tsp salt

Directions:

1. Fit the Cuisinart oven with the rack in position 2.
2. Add all nuts to the air fryer basket then place an air fryer basket in the baking pan.
3. Place a baking pan on the oven rack. Set to air fry at 320 F for 9 minutes.
4. Drizzle nuts with olive oil and season with salt and toss well.
5. Serve and enjoy.

Nutritional Value (Amount per Serving):

- Calories 280
- Fat 29 g
- Carbohydrates 4.9 g
- Sugar 1.3 g
- Protein 4.7 g
- Cholesterol 0 mg

Creamy Chicken Dip

Preparation Time: 10 minutes

Cooking Time: 20 minutes

Serve: 6

Ingredients:

- 2 cups chicken, cooked and shredded
- 8 oz cream cheese, softened
- 3 tbsp hot sauce
- 1/4 tsp garlic powder
- 3/4 cup sour cream
- 1/4 tsp onion powder

Directions:

1. Fit the Cuisinart oven with the rack in position 2.
2. Add all ingredients in a large bowl and mix until well combined.
3. Transfer mixture in air fryer baking dish.
4. Set to bake at 325 F for 25 minutes. After 5 minutes place the baking dish in the preheated oven.
5. Serve and enjoy.

Nutritional Value (Amount per Serving):

- Calories 265
- Fat 20.7 g
- Carbohydrates 2.5 g
- Sugar 0.3 g
- Protein 17.4 g
- Cholesterol 90 mg

Cheddar Dill Mushrooms

Preparation Time: 10 minutes

Cooking Time: 5 minutes

Serve: 6

Ingredients:

- 9 oz mushrooms, cut stems
- 6 oz mozzarella cheese, shredded
- 1 tbsp butter
- 1 tsp dried parsley
- 1/2 tsp salt

Directions:

1. Fit the Cuisinart oven with the rack in position 2.
2. Add parsley, cheese, butter, and salt into the bowl and mix until well combined.
3. Stuff cheese mixture into the mushroom caps and place in the air fryer basket then place an air fryer basket in the baking pan.
4. Place a baking pan on the oven rack. Set to air fry at 400 F for 5 minutes.
5. Serve and enjoy.

Nutritional Value (Amount per Serving):

- Calories 141
- Fat 11.5 g
- Carbohydrates 1.9 g
- Sugar 0.9 g
- Protein 8.5 g
- Cholesterol 35 mg

Chapter 8: Desserts

Easy Almond Butter Pumpkin Spice Cookies

Preparation Time: 10 minutes
Cooking Time: 18 minutes
Serve: 6

Ingredients:

- 1/4 tsp pumpkin pie spice
- 1 tsp liquid Stevie
- 6 oz almond butter
- 1/3 cup pumpkin puree

Directions:

1. Fit the Cuisinart oven with the rack in position 1.
2. Add all ingredients into the food processor and process until just combined.
3. Drop spoonfuls of mixture onto the parchment-lined baking pan.
4. Set to bake at 350 F for 23 minutes. After 5 minutes place the baking pan in the preheated oven.
5. Serve and enjoy.

Nutritional Value (Amount per Serving):

- Calories 85
- Fat 7 g
- Carbohydrates 3 g
- Sugar 1 g
- Protein 3 g
- Cholesterol 0 mg

Walnut Carrot Cake

Preparation Time: 10 minutes

Cooking Time: 25 minutes

Serve: 4

Ingredients:

- 1 egg
- 1/2 cup sugar
- 1/4 cup canola oil
- 1/4 cup walnuts, chopped
- 1/2 tsp baking powder
- 1/2 cup flour
- 1/4 cup grated carrot
- 1/2 tsp vanilla
- 1/2 tsp cinnamon

Directions:

1. Fit the Cuisinart oven with the rack in position 1.
2. In a medium bowl, beat sugar and oil for 1 minute. Add vanilla, cinnamon, and egg and beat for 30 seconds.
3. Add remaining ingredients and stir everything well until just combined.
4. Pour batter into the greased baking dish.
5. Set to bake at 350 F for 30 minutes. After 5 minutes place the baking dish in the preheated oven.
6. Serve and enjoy.

Nutritional Value (Amount per Serving):

- Calories 340
- Fat 20 g
- Carbohydrates 40 g
- Sugar 25 g
- Protein 5 g
- Cholesterol 41 mg

Tasty Almond Macaroons

Preparation Time: 10 minutes

Cooking Time: 10 minutes

Serve: 36

Ingredients:

- 2 egg whites
- 10 oz almonds, sliced
- 1/2 tsp vanilla extract
- 3/4 cup Splenda

Directions:

1. Fit the Cuisinart oven with the rack in position 1.
2. In a bowl, beat egg whites until foamy then add Splenda and vanilla and blend on low.
3. Add almonds in the egg mixture and fold gently.
4. Using a scoop drop out the mixture onto the parchment-lined baking pan.
5. Set to bake at 350 F for 15 minutes. After 5 minutes place the baking pan in the preheated oven.
6. Serve and enjoy.

Nutritional Value (Amount per Serving):

- Calories 67
- Fat 3.9 g
- Carbohydrates 5.7 g
- Sugar 4.4 g
- Protein 1.9 g
- Cholesterol 0 mg

Vanilla Peanut Butter Cake

Preparation Time: 10 minutes

Cooking Time: 30 minutes

Serve: 8

Ingredients:

- 1 1/2 cups all-purpose flour
- 1/3 cup vegetable oil
- 1 tsp baking soda
- 1/2 cup peanut butter powder
- 1 tsp vanilla
- 1 tbsp apple cider vinegar
- 1 cup of water
- 1 cup of sugar
- 1/2 tsp salt

Directions:

1. Fit the Cuisinart oven with the rack in position 1.
2. In a large mixing bowl, mix together flour, baking soda, peanut butter powder, sugar, and salt.
3. In a small bowl, whisk together oil, vanilla, vinegar, and water.
4. Pour oil mixture into the flour mixture and stir until well combined.
5. Pour batter into the greased cake pan.
6. Set to bake at 350 F for 35 minutes. After 5 minutes place the cake pan in the preheated oven.
7. Slice and serve.

Nutritional Value (Amount per Serving):

- Calories 264
- Fat 1.8 g
- Carbohydrates 43.2 g
- Sugar 25.3 g
- Protein 2.6 g
- Cholesterol 0 mg

Chocolate Cake

Preparation Time: 10 minutes

Cooking Time: 30 minutes

Serve: 8

Ingredients:

- 1/2 cup warm water
- 2 3/4 cups flour
- 1 cup buttermilk
- 1 cup shortening
- 1 cup sugar, granulated
- 1 cup brown sugar
- 2 large eggs
- 1/2 cup cocoa powder
- 1 tsp baking soda

Directions:

1. Fit the Cuisinart oven with the rack in position 1.
2. In a large mixing bowl, beat together brown sugar, granulated sugar, and shortening until creamy.
3. Add eggs, cocoa powder, flour, and buttermilk mix well until combine.
4. Dissolve soda in warm water and stir into batter.
5. Pour batter into the greased baking dish.
6. Set to bake at 350 F for 35 minutes. After 5 minutes place the baking dish in the preheated oven.
7. Slices and serve.

Nutritional Value (Amount per Serving):

- Calories 588
- Fat 28.3 g
- Carbohydrates 80.1 g
- Sugar 44.4 g
- Protein 8 g
- Cholesterol 48 mg

Mini Brownie Muffins

Preparation Time: 10 minutes
Cooking Time: 15 minutes
Serve: 6

Ingredients:

- 3 eggs
- 1/2 cup Swerve
- 1 cup almond flour
- 1 tbsp gelatin
- 1/3 cup butter, melted
- 1/3 cup cocoa powder

Directions:

1. Fit the Cuisinart oven with the rack in position 1.
2. Line 6-cups muffin tin with cupcake liners and set aside.
3. Add all ingredients into the mixing bowl and stir until well combined.
4. Pour mixture into the prepared muffin tin.
5. Set to bake at 350 F for 20 minutes. After 5 minutes place muffin tin in the preheated oven.
6. Serve and enjoy.

Nutritional Value (Amount per Serving):

- Calories 163
- Fat 15.4 g
- Carbohydrates 4 g
- Sugar 0.4 g
- Protein 5.8 g
- Cholesterol 109 mg

Vanilla Banana Brownies

Preparation Time: 10 minutes
Cooking Time: 20 minutes
Serve: 12

Ingredients:

- 1 egg
- 1 cup all-purpose flour
- 4 oz white chocolate
- 1/4 cup butter
- 1 tsp vanilla extract
- 1/2 cup granulated sugar
- 2 medium bananas, mashed
- 1/4 tsp salt

Directions:

1. Fit the Cuisinart oven with the rack in position 1.
2. Add white chocolate and butter in a microwave-safe bowl and microwave for 30 seconds. Stir until melted.
3. Stir in sugar. Add mashed bananas, eggs, vanilla, and salt and mix until combined.
4. Add flour and mix until just combined.
5. Pour batter into the greased baking dish.
6. Set to bake at 350 F for 25 minutes. After 5 minutes place the baking dish in the preheated oven.
7. Slice and serve.

Nutritional Value (Amount per Serving):

- Calories 178
- Fat 7.4 g
- Carbohydrates 26.4 g
- Sugar 16.4 g
- Protein 2.3 g
- Cholesterol 26 mg

Flavorful Coconut Cake

Preparation Time: 10 minutes

Cooking Time: 20 minutes

Serve: 8

Ingredients:

- 5 eggs, separated
- 1/2 cup erythritol
- 1/4 cup coconut milk
- 1/2 cup coconut flour
- 1/2 tsp baking powder
- 1/2 tsp vanilla
- 1/2 cup butter softened
- Pinch of salt

Directions:

1. Fit the Cuisinart oven with the rack in position 1.
2. Grease cake pan with butter and set aside.
3. In a bowl, beat sweetener and butter until combined.
4. Add egg yolks, coconut milk, and vanilla and mix well.
5. Add baking powder, coconut flour, and salt and stir well.
6. In another bowl, beat egg whites until stiff peak forms.
7. Gently fold egg whites into the cake mixture.
8. Pour batter in a prepared cake pan.
9. Set to bake at 400 F for 25 minutes. After 5 minutes place the cake pan in the preheated oven.
10. Slice and serve.

Nutritional Value (Amount per Serving):

- Calories 84
- Fat 5.9 g
- Carbohydrates 4.2 g
- Sugar 0.6 g
- Protein 4 g
- Cholesterol 102 mg

Almond Pecan Cookies

Preparation Time: 10 minutes
Cooking Time: 20 minutes
Serve: 16

Ingredients:

- 1/2 cup butter
- 1 tsp vanilla
- 2 tsp gelatin
- 2/3 cup Swerve
- 1 cup pecans
- 1/3 cup coconut flour
- 1 cup almond flour

Directions:

1. Fit the Cuisinart oven with the rack in position 1.
2. Add butter, vanilla, gelatin, swerve, coconut flour, and almond flour into the food processor and process until crumbs form.
3. Add pecans and process until chopped.
4. Make cookies from prepared mixture and place onto a parchment-lined baking pan.
5. Set to bake at 350 F for 25 minutes. After 5 minutes place the baking pan in the preheated oven.
6. Serve and enjoy.

Nutritional Value (Amount per Serving):

- Calories 101
- Fat 10.2 g
- Carbohydrates 1.4 g
- Sugar 0.3 g
- Protein 1.8 g
- Cholesterol 15 mg

Orange Almond Muffins

Preparation Time: 10 minutes
Cooking Time: 20 minutes
Serve: 12

Ingredients:

- 4 eggs
- 1 tsp baking soda
- 1 orange zest
- 1 orange juice
- 1/2 cup butter, melted
- 3 cups almond flour

Directions:

1. Fit the Cuisinart oven with the rack in position 1.
2. Line 12-cups muffin tin with cupcake liners and set aside.
3. Add all ingredients into the large bowl and mix until well combined.
4. Pour mixture into the prepared muffin tin.
5. Set to bake at 350 F for 25 minutes. After 5 minutes place muffin tin in the preheated oven.
6. Serve and enjoy.

Nutritional Value (Amount per Serving):

- Calories 273
- Fat 24 g
- Carbohydrates 6 g
- Sugar 1 g
- Protein 2 g
- Cholesterol 75 mg

Easy Lemon Cheesecake

Preparation Time: 10 minutes

Cooking Time: 55 minutes

Serve: 8

Ingredients:

- 4 eggs
- 2 tbsp swerve
- 1 fresh lemon juice
- 18 oz ricotta cheese
- 1 fresh lemon zest

Directions:

1. Fit the Cuisinart oven with the rack in position 1.
2. In a large bowl, beat ricotta cheese until smooth.
3. Add egg one by one and whisk well.
4. Add lemon juice, lemon zest, and swerve and mix well.
5. Transfer mixture into the greased cake pan.
6. Set to bake at 350 F for 60 minutes. After 5 minutes place the cake pan in the preheated oven.
7. Slice and serve.

Nutritional Value (Amount per Serving):

- Calories 122
- Fat 7.3 g
- Carbohydrates 4.2 g
- Sugar 0.5 g
- Protein 10.1 g
- Cholesterol 102 mg

Delicious Banana Cake

Preparation Time: 10 minutes

Cooking Time: 40 minutes

Serve: 8

Ingredients:

- 2 large eggs, beaten
- 1 tsp baking powder
- 1 1/2 cup sugar, granulated
- 1 tsp vanilla extract
- 1/2 cup butter
- 1 cup milk
- 2 cups all-purpose flour
- 2 bananas, mashed
- 1 tsp baking soda

Directions:

1. Fit the Cuisinart oven with the rack in position 1.
2. In a mixing bowl, beat together sugar and butter until creamy. Add beaten eggs and mix well.
3. Add milk, vanilla extract, baking soda, baking powder, flour, and mashed bananas into the mixture and beat for 2 minutes. Mix well.
4. Pour batter into the greased baking dish.
5. Set to bake at 350 F for 45 minutes. After 5 minutes place the baking dish in the preheated oven.
6. Slices and serve.

Nutritional Value (Amount per Serving):

- Calories 418
- Fat 13.8 g
- Carbohydrates 80 g
- Sugar 42.7 g
- Protein 6.2 g
- Cholesterol 80 mg

Flavors Pumpkin Custard

Preparation Time: 10 minutes
Cooking Time: 40 minutes
Serve: 6

Ingredients:

- 4 egg yolks
- 1/2 tsp cinnamon
- 1 tsp liquid stevia
- 15 oz pumpkin puree
- 3/4 cup coconut cream
- 1/8 tsp cloves
- 1/8 tsp ginger

Directions:

1. Fit the Cuisinart oven with the rack in position 1.
2. In a large bowl, mix together pumpkin puree, cloves, ginger, cinnamon, and swerve.
3. Add egg yolks and beat until well combined.
4. Add coconut cream and stir well.
5. Pour mixture into the six ramekins.
6. Set to bake at 350 F for 45 minutes. After 5 minutes place ramekins in the preheated oven.
7. Serve chilled and enjoy.

Nutritional Value (Amount per Serving):

- Calories 130
- Fat 10.4 g
- Carbohydrates 8 g
- Sugar 3.4 g
- Protein 3.3 g
- Cholesterol 140 mg

Tasty Gingersnap Cookies

Preparation Time: 10 minutes

Cooking Time: 10 minutes

Serve: 8

Ingredients:

- 1 egg
- 1/2 tsp ground cinnamon
- 1/2 tsp ground ginger
- 1 tsp baking powder
- 3/4 cup erythritol
- 1/2 tsp vanilla
- 1/8 tsp ground cloves
- 1/4 tsp ground nutmeg
- 2/4 cup butter, melted
- 1 1/2 cups almond flour
- Pinch of salt

Directions:

1. Fit the Cuisinart oven with the rack in position 1.
2. In a mixing bowl, mix together all dry ingredients.
3. In another bowl, mix together all wet ingredients.
4. Add dry ingredients to the wet ingredients and mix until a dough-like mixture is formed.
5. Cover and place in the refrigerator for 30 minutes.
6. Make cookies from dough and place onto a parchment-lined baking pan.
7. Set to bake at 350 F for 15 minutes. After 5 minutes place the baking pan in the preheated oven.
8. Serve and enjoy.

Nutritional Value (Amount per Serving):

- Calories 142
- Fat 14.7 g
- Carbohydrates 1.8 g
- Sugar 0.3 g
- Protein 2 g
- Cholesterol 51 mg

Strawberry Muffins

Preparation Time: 10 minutes

Cooking Time: 20 minutes

Serve: 12

Ingredients:

- 4 eggs
- 1/4 cup water
- 1/2 cup butter, melted
- 2 tsp baking powder
- 2 cups almond flour
- 2/3 cup strawberries, chopped
- 2 tsp vanilla
- 1/4 cup erythritol
- Pinch of salt

Directions:

1. Fit the Cuisinart oven with the rack in position 1.
2. Line 12-cups muffin tin with cupcake liners and set aside.
3. In a medium bowl, mix together almond flour, baking powder, and salt.
4. In a separate bowl, whisk eggs, sweetener, vanilla, water, and butter.
5. Add almond flour mixture into the egg mixture and mix until well combined.
6. Add strawberries and stir well.
7. Pour batter into the prepared muffin tin.
8. Set to bake at 350 F for 25 minutes. After 5 minutes place muffin tin in the preheated oven.
9. Serve and enjoy.

Nutritional Value (Amount per Serving):

- Calories 201
- Fat 18.5 g
- Carbohydrates 5.2 g
- Sugar 1.3 g
- Protein 6 g
- Cholesterol 75 mg

Conclusion

Convection toaster ovens aren't just for professional kitchens—now you can enjoy everything you would from a restaurant right in your own home with this Cuisinart Chef's Convection Toaster Oven Cookbook. From Mouth-Watering breakfast to perfectly dinner, here's how to get the most out of your Cuisinart Convection Toaster Oven—no experience required.

With this Cuisinart Chef's Convection Toaster Oven Cookbook, you'll learn the science behind convection cooking and how these special ovens can make your favorite dishes even tastier. Then, combine your newfound knowledge of best practices with 1000-Day creative, tasty recipes and see why everyone raves about the crispy, tender, and flavorful meals that convection toaster ovens yield.

www.ingramcontent.com/pod-product-compliance
Lightning Source LLC
Chambersburg PA
CBHW081402070526
44583CB00020B/2640